Insignia, Rank and Badges of the U. S. Army Vietnam

Dedicated to all Vietnam veterans and their families who supported them when they so unselfishly served their country in the United States Army.

Ebook Edition ISBN - 978-1-884452-23-9
Softcover Edition ISBN - 978-1-884452-36-9

Copyright 2024 by MOA Press

All rights reserved. No part of this publication may be reproduced, stored in retrieval systems or transmitted by any means, electronic, mechanical or by photocopying, recording or by any information storage and retrieval system without permission from the publisher, except for the inclusion of brief quotations in a review.

Press
Published by:

MOA Press (Medals of America Press)
325 Rocky Slope Road, Suite 104-234
Greenville, SC 29607
www.moapress.com • www.usmedals.com

MOA Press (Medals of America Press)
114 Southchase Blvd.
Fountain Inn, SC 29644
www.moapress.com • www.usmedals.com

Insignia, Rank and Badges of the U. S. Army Vietnam

Table of Contents

Introduction	3
Army Branch Insignia	8
Army Officer and Enlisted Branch Insignia	10
Army Branch Insignia shown alphabetically	11
Officer and Enlisted Rank Insignia	24
Hat Badges, Buttons and Lapel Insignia	30
Army Badges and Tabs	32-47

COL. FRANK C. FOSTER *(Ret.)*, obtained his BS from The Citadel, MBA from the University of Georgia and is a graduate of the Army's Command and General Staff College and War College. He saw service as a Battery Commander in Germany and served in Vietnam with the 173rd Airborne Brigade and USARV General Staff. In the Adjutant General's Corps, he served as the Adjutant General of the Central Army Group, the 4th Infantry Division and was the Commandant and Chief of the Army's Adjutant General's Corps from 1986 to 1990. His military service provided him a unique understanding of the Armed Forces Awards System. He currently operates Medals of America Press and is the author of the *Military Medals of America, U.S. Army Medals, Badges and Insignia, Medals and Insignia of the Republic of Vietnam* and numerous books on the Air Force, Marines and Navy awards. He and his wife Linda, who was decorated with the Army Commander's Medal in 1990 for service to the Army, live in Greenville, South Carolina.

The story of our Army during the Vietnam war through its symbols of valor, professional skill and identification.

Introduction

"*Over* 1,700,000 U.S. Army soldiers have served in Vietnam. This book tells the story of the military awards they earned and the military insignia they worn that identifed them."

In 1957, the North Vietnamese led Vietcong began a rebellion against the South Vietnam government whom the U.S. supported with equipment and advisors. In August 1964, Congress passed the Tonkin Gulf Resolution giving the President the power to take "all necessary measures" to "prevent further (Communist) aggression." Between 1965 and 1969, US troop strength rose from 60,000 to over 543,000 in country. With the infusion of American arms, advice and training, the Army of the Republic of Vietnam (ARVN) and the Regional Forces and Popular Forces (RF/PF) steadily improved. The enthusiastic American units, however, tended to push the Army of South Vietnam (ARVN) aside to get into battle, a situation the ARVN, knowing it was a long war, was pleased to accept. In 1969 when the United States decided to start winding down their support in the war, the ARVN had not built up the requisite experience and confidence. The ARVN officers corps and commanders varied too widely in quality. Nevertheless many of the ARVN units, ranging from the Airborne to individual Regional Forces (RF) companies, were excellent. The Republic of South Vietnam armed forces were in combat during most of the republic's life, at times with valor and success, but in the end not with victory. The United States aided by others came to the defense of the Republic of Vietnam in an intervention but in the end failed. American forces lost no battles, but the cost grew to high in blood, money and politics.

So putting aside the thousands of articles written by people who were not there, the war was fought with a clear mission of defending a free country against a communist invasion …and it was fought bravely and successfully by a force of mostly American and South Vietnamese troops until the January 1973 Paris Peace Agreements. Based on the Peace Agreement U.S. forces withdrew from South Vietnam.

After the 1973 "Peace Agreement", the Army of South Vietnam (ARVN) and the People's Army of North Vietnam (PAVN) jostled for territory. In January 1975, North Vietnamese seized Phuoc Long province. When this did not bring about a United States reaction, the People's Army of North Vietnam went ahead with plans for a major offensive. After grinding and inconclusive combat north of Hue in early 1975, the People's Army of North Vietnam attacked Banmethuot in the Highlands in March. President Thieu decided to abandon the Highlands and also withdraw the Airborne Division from Central Vietnam for use as a reserve. While perhaps strategically sound, the moves provoked panic, and South Vietnam crumbled. A last-minute peace government of General Duong Van Minh was contemptuously swept aside by the victors and the Republic of Vietnam died twenty years after it was founded.

The American military was not defeated by North Vietnam's final 1975 blitzkrieg for the simple reason that there were no American military forces there to be defeated. They had left country years earlier. Ironically, that irrefutable historical fact does not seem to have registered on many Americans who still talk about America's military defeat in Vietnam. They are entitled to their own set of opinions but, as former Secretary of Defense James Schlesinger once observed, "they are not entitled to their own set of facts when it comes to shooting down Vietnam War myths, and facts".

So this book is written for United States Army Vietnam veterans and their families in an effort to help them identify and display the military insignia and badges that represent their service in Vietnam. The majority of the Army Vietnam veterans were volunteers and were joined by many young men who answered their countries call when drafted.

Of the 3,400,000 million Americans that served in the United States Armed Forces during the Vietnam War, the majority served in the United States Army. This book tells the story of the the skills they developed and the military insignia they served under. The book is not just for Vietnam veterans, but also for veterans' families. When all is said and done, it is more important for a soldier's family to gain an appreciation for the dedication and skill which went into earning these insignia.

It is the story of our Army during the Vietnam war through its symbols of professional skill and responsibilty. Every effort has been made to provide the criteria and background for each insignia and badge. However, when it came to the area of shoulder sleeve insignia or patches, Major Peter Morgan has done a superb job of covering the wide variety of shoulder sleeve insignia in his book, (*The United States Military Patch Guide*).

From the first day in the Army, every soldier begins to earn a branch of service and rank insignia which indicates a skill and responsibility. For over 230 years the United States Army has developed its own unique uniform system of a soldier specialty (combat arms, combat support or combat service support) Initially it was colors, a different color and unique insignia for each branch of the service as well as insignia on uniform to indicate the individual soldiers rank and responsibility from general to private.

In the Civil War unique insignia was designated to identify individual soldiers with their units. World War I introduced individual shoulder sleeve insignia or patches for every major unit. World War II saw different badges awarded soldiers to indicate special skills or combat experience.

So the purpose of this book is to bring together the story and symbolism of the insignia and military badges and rank insignia the Vietnam veteran may have earned. The United States Army insignia and badges that recognize and identify a Vietnam veterans service.

Your book starts with the soldiers first insignia, their branch of service *(Infantry, Artillery, Armor or one of the many other branches of the army)*. It then walks you through Army rank insignia and combat and skill badges. Finally, as hard as we try, we know there will be mistakes in this book. Therefore please send all comments, suggestions and corrections in care of the publisher. Thank you for using this book. In so doing, you honor the memory of great Americans, our Army veterans. **"Let no veteran be forgotten!"**

Frank Foster,

173rd Airborne Brigade

1967-68

Branch Insignia

During the Revolutionary War, there were no standardized branch insignia as the Army was in its infancy. Soldiers typically wore uniform distinctions such as cockades or colored facings to indicate their regiment or unit affiliation. Officers were distinguished by their rank insignia, typically worn on epaulets or shoulder straps. Enlisted personnel had few visual indicators of branch or specialization.

In the early 19th century, the U.S. Army began organizing into specialized branches such as Infantry, Cavalry, Artillery, and Engineers. However, formal branch insignia did not yet exist. Officers continued to be distinguished by their rank insignia and often by the type of uniform they wore. Enlisted personnel were identified primarily by their regiment or company.

The Civil War saw the emergence of more standardized branch insignia for officers, particularly in the Union Army. Officers began wearing insignia on their shoulder straps or collar points to denote their branch. Enlisted personnel still lacked branch insignia but were identified by their regimental affiliation or specific unit patches.

By World War I, branch insignia for officers had become more established, with symbols such as crossed rifles for Infantry and crossed cannons for Artillery. Enlisted personnel began to wear distinctive branch insignia on their collar devices or hat pins, although these were not as widespread or standardized as they are today. During World War II, branch insignia became more widely adopted and standardized for both officers and enlisted personnel. This period saw the introduction of many of the branch insignia still in use today. Soldiers wore their branch insignia prominently on their uniform lapels or collars, helping to identify their specialization and role within the Army.

In the post-World War II era and leading into the Vietnam War, branch insignia continued to be an integral part of Army uniforms, symbolizing a soldier's expertise and specialization. The design of branch insignia evolved to reflect changes in military technology and doctrine, with new branches such as Aviation and Special Forces being established after the Vietnam War.

During the Vietnam War United States Army branch insignia denoted a soldier's primary area of expertise or assignment within the Army. These insignias were worn on the Army Uniform and serve several purposes, including indicating a soldier's branch or specialty, fostering esprit de corps, and promoting unit cohesion.

The idea behind branch insignia is to provide visual identification of a soldier's role within the Army. Branch insignia help identify a soldier's primary job function or specialty within the Army. For example, the Infantry branch insignia features crossed muskets, symbolizing the primary weapon of infantry soldiers, while the Medical Corps insignia includes a caduceus, representing medical expertise.

Many branch insignia incorporate symbols and imagery that hold historical significance or represent the core values of the branch. For example, the Quartermaster Corps insignia features a key and a sword, symbolizing the Corps' role in providing logistical support and sustaining the Army's operations. Branch insignia serve as outward symbols of a soldier's expertise and professionalism in their respective fields. They signify the specialized training and skills required to perform effectively within a particular branch of the Army.

United States Army branch insignia play a crucial role in identifying soldiers' roles, fostering unit cohesion, recognizing expertise and achievements, and preserving the traditions and values of the Army's various branches.

During the Vietnam War, United States Army branch insignia were worn on various uniforms depending on the type of uniform and the soldier's rank. On the Class A Service Uniform, officers wore their branch insignia on both collars of the coat, positioned approximately 1 inch from the front edge and centered vertically between the top and bottom edges of the collar. Enlisted personnel wore their branch insignia on both collars of the coat as well, but positioned so that the bottom of the insignia was 1 inch from the lower edge of the collar and centered horizontally. Similar to the OG-107 Fatigue Uniform, officers wore subdued metal pin-on branch insignia on the left collar of the shirt of the Jungle Fatigues. Enlisted personnel also wore subdued metal rank pin-on insignia on both collars of the shirt but no branch insignia on the combat uniform. Special Forces soldiers often wore distinctive berets as part of their uniform. Some would typically wear their branch insignia on the flash (patch) on the front of the beret, which denoted their Special Forces affiliation. Overall, during the Vietnam War, United States Army branch insignia were worn on various uniforms in accordance with regulations, serving to identify a soldier's branch or specialty.

Rank Insignia

The use of rank insignia in the United States Army has evolved significantly since the Revolutionary War, reflecting changes in military organization, command structure, and uniform regulations. During the Revolutionary War, officers were typically distinguished by the style and quality of their uniforms, as well as by their actions on the battlefield. High-ranking officers might wear epaulets or gorgets as symbols of their authority. Enlisted men had few visual indicators of rank, with distinctions such as chevrons or cockades sometimes worn on their uniforms, though these were not standardized across the army.

In the early 19th century, the U.S. Army began to adopt more formal rank insignia for officers. These often consisted of epaulets, shoulder straps, or collar devices bearing symbols such as stars or bars to denote rank. Enlisted men began to wear chevrons on their sleeves or cuffs to indicate their rank, with the number and arrangement of chevrons varying depending on the specific rank. During the Civil War, rank insignia became more standardized and widely used. Officers of the Union Army wore shoulder straps with various combinations of stars, bars, and eagles to denote their rank. Enlisted men continued to wear chevrons on their sleeves, with the number of chevrons indicating rank.

In the late 19th and early 20th centuries, the U.S. Army continued to refine its system of rank insignia. Officers' insignia typically featured more elaborate designs, often incorporating elements such as oak leaves or crossed sabers to denote specific branches or specialties. Enlisted rank insignia remained relatively consistent, with chevrons indicating rank and additional elements such as arcs or rockers sometimes added to signify non-commissioned officer (NCO) status.

By World War I, rank insignia for both officers and enlisted men had become more standardized and widely recognized. Officers' insignia typically featured metal pins worn on the collar or shoulder straps, while enlisted rank insignia were worn on the sleeves. The ranks of warrant officers, introduced during this period, were denoted by unique insignia typically featuring a combination of bars and arcs. Today, officers' rank insignia typically consist of metal pins worn on the collar or epaulets, while enlisted personnel wear cloth patches or pins on the sleeves of their uniforms. Warrant officers' insignia have also evolved, with distinctive designs denoting their rank and specialty.

Throughout U.S. military history, rank insignia have played a crucial role in maintaining order, discipline, and the chain of command within the Army. They serve as visual indicators of a soldier's authority, expertise, and responsibilities, helping to ensure effective leadership and coordination in times of peace and war.

Badges

During the Vietnam War, United States Army qualification, skill, combat badges and identification badges held significant importance for soldiers. These badges served various purposes, including recognizing individual proficiency, enhancing unit cohesion, and symbolizing combat experience.

Of the key badges used during the Vietnam War, the Combat Infantryman Badge was one of the most prestigious badges awarded. It was presented to infantrymen who actively participated in ground combat against the enemy. The Combat Medical Badge represents the bravery and selflessness of medical personnel in providing care under fire and was awarded to medics and other medical personnel who provided medical care to wounded soldiers while under enemy fire or in a combat zone.

The Parachutist Badge symbolizes the soldier's training, skill, and readiness to conduct airborne operations behind enemy lines. It was awarded to soldiers who successfully completed airborne training and made qualifying parachute jumps. The Ranger Tab signifies the soldier's mastery of small-unit tactics, leadership skills, and ability to operate in challenging environments. It is a symbol of elite combat proficiency.

These badges were not only symbols of individual achievement but also fostered unit pride and cohesion. They were worn with honor by soldiers who had demonstrated exceptional skill, bravery, and dedication in combat or specialized training. During the Vietnam War, these badges became iconic symbols of the courage and sacrifice of American soldiers in the face of adversity.

The United States Army also utilized various badges to recognize marksmanship proficiency, aviation qualifications, identification, and specialized skills. These badges played important roles in acknowledging soldiers' abilities, fostering unit cohesion, and symbolizing expertise. These badges served as visible symbols of soldiers' training, expertise, and accomplishments. They provided recognition for individual skills, promoted esprit de corps within units, and helped to identify soldiers' roles and capabilities on the battlefield. During the Vietnam War, these badges were worn with pride by soldiers who demonstrated excellence in their respective fields, contributing to the overall effectiveness and success of U.S. military operations.

Introduction to Army Branch Insignia

From the time of the Revolution, the Army has been organized into traditional European branches of service such as Infantry, Artillery, Cavalry, Ordnance, Adjutant General, Medical, etc.

Since World War II, the Army branches have become identified in three groups - Combat Arms, Combat Support and Combat Service Support. There are several branches or detailed branches which technically do not fit in any of these categories but for the purpose of this book, they are considered Combat Service Support. During the Vietnam War there were 29 branches in the Army, depending on how you count them.

The Combat Arms branches were: Infantry, Field Artillery, Air Defense Artillery, Armor, and Corps of Engineers. Aviation did not become a basic branch of the Army until 1983 and Special Forces until 1987. During the Vietnam War personnel in those units worn their basic branch insignia.

The Combat Support branches were: Signal Corps, Military Police, Chemical Corps, and Military Intelligence Corps.

The Combat Service Support branches were: Adjutant General's Corps, Chaplain Corps, Finance Corps, Judge Advocate General's Corps, Ordnance Corps, Quartermaster Corps, Transportation Corps, Medical Corps, Dental Corps, Veterinary Corps, Medical Service Corps, Army Nurse Corps, Army Medical Specialist Corps and Army Bands.

The Combat Arms are trained and responsible for actual combat against enemy forces. The Combat Support arms provide operational and technical support to the combat arms and must be prepared to engage in combat if necessary. The Combat Service Support forces main mission is to provide administrative and logistical support to the entire force. These branches normally are not expected to engage in combat but since many soldiers in these branches such as the Adjutant General's Corps, Transportation Corps and Ordnance Corps plus others can be assigned to combat arms units, they must be trained in combat operations.

Additionally there are detailed special branches such as the General Staff and Inspector General to which select officers are assigned for periods of duty. The U.S. Army Reserve has two branches; Civil Affairs and Staff Specialist *(which folds into other branches upon mobilization)*.

Every book has to start somewhere and every soldiers service began by being assigned to a specific branch in the Army so that is where we will start. We will take a look at each one of the branches of the Army followed by the Army's enlisted and officer rank system and the Army system of skill, qualification and identification badges.

Every officer, warrant officer and enlisted soldier who entered the Army during the Vietnam War was trained to serve in a specific branch of the Army. Each of the branches authorized during the period of the Vietnam War was symbolized by the means of a distinctive unit insignia worn on the lapel or collars of a soldier's uniform. The various branches of the Army were grouped into four categories: the Combat Arms, composed of Infantry, Field Artillery, Air Defense Artillery, Armor, Special Forces, and Corps of Engineers.

The second category we visit are the Combat Support branches and these included: Signal Corps, Military Police, Chemical Corps, and Military Intelligence Corps. The third category composed the Combat Service Support branches, these were: Adjutant General's Corps, Chaplain Corps, Finance Corps, Judge Advocate General's Corps, Ordnance Corps, Quartermaster Corps, Transportation Corps Civil Affairs and Warrant Officers Corps. The special branches of the Army made up the final category and was composed of the Medical Corps, the Dental Corps, Medical Service Corps, the Army Nurses Corps and the Army Medical Specialist Corps. There were also four specialty detailed branches which were the General Staff detail, the Inspector General, the National Guard Bureau, Staff specialist for the Army National Guard and US Army Reserve and perhaps the most special of all the Army branches: Army Bands.

On page 10 examples of all of the officer and enlisted branch insignia are shown in alphabetical order. The following pages provide short descriptions of all of these branches and the heraldry behind them. These are also listed in alphabetical order just to make them easier to find in reference instead of groupings by combat arms, combat support, combat service support and special branches.

Every soldier arrived in Vietnam wearing a U.S. and branch insignia. In this example a young Infantry PFC is wearing a US and Infantry disk on his right and left collar along with the special Infantry Blue cord on his right shoulder. His unit crests (if he had them yet) were worn on his epaulets and his rank (in this case a Private First Class) is worn on both sleeves. Over his right pocket is a name tag and over his left pocket is a National Defense Service Ribbon with Expert and Sharpshooters Qualification Badges below.

The U.S. disk is a direct decendent of the first official U.S. Army insignia.. USA buttons worn on the uniform of American Revolutionary Soldiers, a tradtion carried on for over 200 years.

Revolutionary uniform buttons and a World War One collar disk.

Medals of America Press 9

Officer and Enlisted Branch Insignia — Listed Alphabetically

| Adjutant General's Corps | Air Defense Artillery | Armor | Cavalry |

Army Band

Chaplains Corps

Christian — Jewish (1) Old Version — Enlisted Chaplains Assistant

Chemical Corps — Civil Affairs

Engineers — Field Artillery — Finance Corps — General Staff Detail

Infantry — Infantry with blue backing disk — Inspector General — Judge Advocate General's Corps

Medical — Dental — Veterinary — Nurse — Specialist — Medical Service Corps

Military Intelligence — Military Police — National Guard Bureau — Ordnance Corps

Quartermaster Corps — Signal Corps — Staff Specialist, ARNG/USAR — Transportation Corps

Warrant Officer Branch — U.S. Enlisted

10 Insignia, Rank and Badges, U.S. Army Vietnam

⭐ Adjutant General's Corps

Old red, white and blue enamel Insignia

Branch Insignia Current

Enlisted Insignia

The **Adjutant General's Corps** serve at all organization levels of the Army where they plan, develop, and operate the Army's personnel management systems such as personnel requisitioning, reassignments, evaluations, promotions, awards and decorations, reenlistment, casualty reporting, strength accounting, and replacement operations. Administrative systems includes courier and postal services.

Branch Insignia: A silver metal and enamel shield 1 inch in height on which are thirteen vertical stripes, 7 silver and 6 red; on a blue chief 1 large and 12 small silver stars.

The basic design, the shield from the Coat of Arms of the United States, was adopted in 1872 as a solid shield of silver, bearing thirteen stars. In 1924, this design was authorized to be made in gold metal with the colors red, white, and blue in enamel. In December 1964, the insignia was changed to silver base metal with silver stars and silver and red enamel stripes.

Branch Colors: Dark blue piped with Scarlet.

Birthday: 16 June 1775. The post of Adjutant General was established 16 June 1775 and has been continuously in operation since that time. The Adjutant General's Department, by that name, was established by the act of 3 March 1813 and was redesignated The Adjutant General's Corps in 1950.

⭐ Air Defense Artillery

Branch Insignia

Enlisted Insignia

Each ADA Regiment has its own regimental insignia and coat of arms.

Air Defense Artillery deploys weapons in support of military land combat operations and against enemy aircraft and missile attacks. Depending upon the mission, Air Defense Artillery units are found defending the ground-gaining combat arms units or critical units/areas against enemy air attack.

Branch Insignia: A missile surmounting two crossed field guns, all of gold colored metal, 1 1/8 inches in height.

Crossed cannons *(field guns)* for Artillery has been in continuous use since 1834, when they were placed on regimental colors, knapsacks, and as part of the cap insignia for Artillery officers.

This insignia was superseded on 2 January 1957 by a new insignia consisting of crossed field guns surmounted by a missile, all gold.

On 20 June 1968, Air Defense Artillery was established as a basic branch of the Army and on 1 December 1968, the ADA branch was authorized to retain the former Artillery insignia, crossed field guns with missile.

Branch Colors: Scarlet. The uniform for the Corps of Artillery, which was formed in 1777, included red trimmings. Scarlet has been the color of the Artillery throughout the history of the branch. Scarlet has been used by the Coast, Field, and Air Defense Artillery.

Birthday: 17 November 1775. The Continental Congress unanimously elected Henry Knox *"Colonel of the Regiment of Artillery"* on 17 November 1775. The regiment formally entered service on 1 January 1776. Although Field Artillery and Air Defense Artillery are separate branches, both inherit the traditions of the Artillery branch.

Medals of America Press

 Armor

Branch Insignia   **Enlisted Insignia**

Armor employs the Armor/Cavalry maneuver forces and combined arms to close with and destroy the enemy using fire, maneuver, and shock action. Armor is called the Combat Arm of Decision.

Branch Insignia: The front view of an M-26 tank, gun slightly raised, superimposed on two crossed Cavalry sabers in scabbards, cutting edge up, 13/16 inch in height overall, of gold color metal.

The Armor insignia, approved in 1950, consists of the traditional crossed sabers *(originally adopted for the cavalry in 1851)* on which the M-26 tank is superimposed. The design symbolizes the traditional and current roles of armor.

Regimental Insignia: Personnel assigned to the Armor branch affiliate with a specific regiment and wear the insignia of the affiliated regiment.

Branch Colors: Yellow. In March 1855, two regiments of cavalry were created and their trimmings were to be of *"yellow."* In 1861, the designation of Dragoon and mounted rifleman disappeared, all becoming Cavalry with *"yellow"* as their colors. Armor was assigned the colors green and white by circular 49 on 21 February 1947. When the Cavalry branch was abolished, the present Armor was assigned the former Cavalry color yellow by SR 600-60-1 dated 26 October 1951.

Birthday: 12 December 1775. The Armor branch traces its origin to the Cavalry. A regiment of Cavalry was authorized to be raised by the Continental Congress Resolve of 12 December 1775. Although mounted units were raised at various times after the Revolution, the first unit in continuous service was the United States Regiment of Dragoons, organized in 1833. The Tank Service was formed 5 March 1918. The Armored Force was formed on 10 July 1940 and became a permanent branch of the Army in 1950.

 Cavalry

Collar Insignia   **Enlisted Insignia**

U.S. Cavalry. The Cavalry branch transitioned to the Armored Forces with tanks in 1940, but the term "cavalry", e.g. "armored cavalry", remains in use in the U.S. Army for mounted (ground and aviation) reconnaissance, surveillance, and target acquisition (RSTA) units based on their parent Combat Arms Regimental System (CARS) regiment

Collar Insignia: Two crossed sabers in scabbards, cutting edge up, 11/16 inch in height, of gold color metal.

The Cavalry insignia was adopted in 1851. Today, officers and enlisted personnel assigned to Cavalry regiments, Cavalry squadrons or separate Cavalry troops are authorized to wear the Cavalry collar insignia in lieu of their insignia of branch when approved by the Major Army commander. Some of the armor and aviation units are designated cavalry units.

Regimental Insignia: Personnel assigned to Cavalry units affiliate with a specific regiment of their branch or cavalry unit and wear the insignia of the affiliated regiment.

Regimental Coat of Arms: Each Cavalry regiment has its own coat of arms that is displayed on the breast of a displayed eagle. The background of all Cavalry flags is yellow.

Colors: Although Cavalry is not a branch, yellow is used as a branch color for personnel assigned to cavalry units. In March 1855, two regiments of Cavalry were created and their trimmings were to be "yellow." In 1861, the designation of Dragoon and Mounted Rifleman disappeared, all becoming Cavalry with "yellow" as their colors.

Yellow was continued as the color for Cavalry units subsequent to abolishment as a branch. Although the regimental flags for Cavalry units are yellow, the troop guidons are red and white without an insignia on the guidon.

⭐ Army Band (Enlisted Only)

Enlisted Insignia

Army Bands: The United States Army has maintained military bands for over two centuries of service. Bands provides musical support for military camps and bases, military areas, and communities across the United States and other territories such as Puerto Rico. Army Bands also serve in Army units outside the country and in regions such as Western Europe or Eastern Asia. There were 8 Army Bands serving in Vietnam by 1969.

Branch Insignia: A lyre, on a one inch disk, all in gold color metal. Enlisted only. In 1950, Special Services *(including bands)* became a responsibility of The Adjutant General. Commissioned and warrant officers serving in Army Bands wear Adjutant General Insignia.

Branch Colors: Old Glory Blue.

⭐ Chaplains Corps

Christian   **Jewish**   **Enlisted Chaplains Assistant**

Chaplains Corps: The Chaplains Branch is a special branch which has the primary mission to perform or provide for comprehensive religious support for soldiers and their family members in war and peace. Chaplains assist commanders in facilitating the right to free exercise of religion for all personnel. Chaplains are commissioned officers and accredited clergy endorsed by a recognized denomination or faith group for the military ministry.

Branch Insignia: Christian Faith: A silver color Latin Cross, one inch in height. The insignia was adopted in 1898.

Jewish Faith: A double tablet bearing Hebrew characters from 1 to 10 surmounted by The Star of David, all of silver color, one inch in height. The insignia for chaplains of the Jewish faith was adopted in 1918 and had Roman numerals on the tablet. The Roman numerals were changed to Hebrew characters on 9 November 1981.

Branch Colors: Black - cloth 65018; yarn 67138, PMS Black. Chaplains have used black since 1835. In regulations dated that year, a black coat was prescribed for Chaplains.

Birthday: 29 July 1775.

⭐ Chemical Corps

Branch Insignia   **Enlisted Insignia**

Chemical Corps: The Chemical Corps encompassesd functions which are primarily oriented toward operations, training, scientific development, and acquisition activities in support of nuclear, biological, chemical (NBC) defense program. The Chemical Corps provides the Army with a highly trained corps of NBC defense and operational experts.

Branch Insignia: A benzene ring of cobalt blue enamel superimposed in the center of crossed gold color retorts, 1/2 inch in height and 1-13/16 inches in width overall. The insignia (in bronze metal) was originally adopted in 1917 for the Chemical Service. In 1921, this insignia was approved for the Chemical Warfare Service. In 1924, the ring was changed to cobalt blue enamel. The benzene ring is the starting point for the method of indicating diagrammatically a molecular composition of the composition of the chemical combination. It has six points, one for each atom of carbon and hydrogen since the formula for benzene is C_6H_6. The retort is the basic container other than the test tube, for laboratory experiments.

Gold and blue, are the colors of the Chemical Corps,

Birthday: 28 June 1918.

Medals of America Press

Civil Affairs

Civil Affairs: In 1955, The Civil Affairs and Military Government Branch, USAR, was established. On 30 April 1956, the Office of Civil Affairs and Military Government gave concurrence in the design *(gold global background with gold torch, sword and scroll superimposed thereon)*. The Department of the Army General Staff approved the design on 1 June 1956. The branch was redesignated to Civil Affairs USAR on 2 October 1959. The globe indicates the worldwide areas of Civil Affairs operations. The torch is from the Statue of Liberty, a symbol associated with the spirit of the United States. It also represents the enlightened performance of duty. The scroll and sword depict the civil and military aspects of the organization's mission. The insignia was authorized for wear by all personnel assigned to Regular Army Civil Affairs TOE units on 13 October 1961.

The only three Civil Affairs *(CA)* companies to serve in the Republic of Vietnam *(RVN)* were the the 2nd, 29th and 41st from 1965 to 1970. Their mission was to bolster faith in the RVN government by helping to *"win the hearts and minds"* of the rural population by assisting with construction, agricultural, medical, economic, and educational programs to improve standards of living. These efforts helped end the Viet Cong's ability to recruit in Southern Vietnam as well as recruit indigenous tribes to take up arms against the Viet Cong and the northern Vietnamese army.

Branch Insignia   **Enlisted Insignia**

Branch Insignia: On a globe 5/8 inch in diameter, a torch of liberty 1 inch in height surmounted by a scroll and a sword crossed in saltire, all of gold color.

Branch Colors: Purple piped with white. Purple - 65009 cloth; 67115 yarn; PMS 267. White - 65005 cloth; 67101 yarn; PMS white. The colors were approved for Civil Affairs units in June 1956.

Birthday: 17 August 1955.

Corps of Engineers

Corps of Engineers: The Corps of Engineers is a Combat Arms Branch which also has combat support and combat service support roles. Engineer officers plan and execute missions relating to engineer support on the battlefield in light, heavy, airborne, and topographic missions. They coordinate and control all facilities and housing support at military installations. Additionally, the engineer officer serves as the Army's component to the Department of Defense *(DOD)* team charged with mapping, charting, geodesy, and military geographic responsibilities.

Branch Insignia: A gold color triple turreted castle eleven-sixteenth inch in height.

The triple turreted castle has been in use by the Corps of Engineers since it was adopted in 1840. Prior to that time a similar insignia was worn on the uniforms of the United States Military Academy Cadets since they were under the direction of the Chief of

Branch Insignia   **Enlisted Insignia**

Engineers. Selection of the turreted castle as the Engineer insignia followed the first major construction undertaken by the Corps of Engineers - the building of a system of castle-like fortifications for the protection of Atlantic Coast harbors. These fortifications, many of which are still standing, were in fact called "castles". By 1924, the insignia had evolved into its current design and gold color.

Branch Colors: Scarlet piped with white. Scarlet - 65006 cloth; 67111 yarn; PMS 200. White - 65005 cloth; 67101 yarn; PMS white. Scarlet and white were established as the Corps of Engineers colors in 1872. Before that date, several other colors had been associated with the Engineers.

Birthday: 16 June 1775. Continental Congress authority for a *"Chief of Engineer for the Army"* dates from 16 June 1775.

Field Artillery

Field Artillery: Field Artillery is the King of Battle. The Field Artillery is one of the Army's combat arms, traditionally one of the three major branches with Infantry and Armor. It refers to those units that use artillery weapons systems to deliver surface-to-surface long range indirect fire. They are experts in the capabilities of cannons, rockets, missiles, naval gunfire, and close air support.

Branch Insignia: Two crossed field guns, gold color metal, thirteen-sixteenth inch in height.

Branch Insignia   Enlisted Insignia

(Each Field Artillery Regiment has its own regimental insignia and coat of arms)

Crossed cannons *(field guns)* for Artillery have been in continuous use since 1834 when they were placed on regimental colors, knapsacks, and as part of the cap insignia for Artillery officers. In 1901, the Artillery was divided into Coast and Field Artillery and the branch insignia was modified by the addition of a plain scarlet oval at the intersection of the cannons. The Field Artillery insignia approved on 17 July 1902 had a gold wheel on the red oval and the Coast Artillery had a gold projectile on the red oval. This red oval and wheel was replaced on 4 April 1907 by two field guns. It was superseded in 1957 by the consolidated Artillery insignia consisting of the crossed field guns surmounted by a missile. In 1968, when the Air Defense Artillery and the Field Artillery were authorized to have separate insignia, the former Field Artillery insignia was reinstated.

Regimental Insignia: Personnel assigned to the Field Artillery branch affiliate with a specific regiment and wear the insignia of the affiliated regiment.

Regimental Coat of Arms: There is no standard Field Artillery regimental flag to represent all of the Field Artillery regiments. Each regiment of Field Artillery has its own coat of arms that appears on the breast of a displayed eagle. The background of all the Field Artillery regimental flags is scarlet with yellow fringe.

Branch Colors: Scarlet - 65006 cloth; 67111 yarn; PMS 200.

The uniform for the Corps of Artillery, which was formed in 1777, included red trimmings. The plume on the hat was also red. Except for a short period at the beginning of the 1800's when yellow was combined with it, scarlet has been the color of the Artillery throughout the history of the branch. Scarlet has been used by the Coast Artillery, Air Defense Artillery and Field Artillery.

Birthday: 17 November 1775. Field Artillery and Air Defense Artillery are separate branches and both inherit the traditions of the Artillery branch.

Finance Corps

Finance Corps: Finance Corps is a combat service support (CSS) branch of the United States Army. It is responsible for financial operations, most notably payroll and resource management.

Branch Insignia   Enlisted Insignia

Branch Insignia: A gold color diamond, 1 inch by 3/4 inch, short axis vertical. In 1896, the diamond design *(embroidered in silver or made of silver metal)* was approved as the insignia of the Pay Department. **Branch Colors:** Silver gray piped with golden yellow.

Birthday: 16 June 1775. The Finance Corps is the successor to the old Pay Department, which was created in June 1775. The Finance Department was created by law on 1 July 1920 and became the Finance Corps in 1950.

⭐ General Staff Detail

Branch Insignia: The coat of arms of the United States, 5/8 inch in height, of gold color metal superimposed on a five-pointed silver color star, 1 inch in circumscribing diameter. The shield to be in enamel stripes of white and red, chief of blue and the glory blue.

The Chief of Staff of the Army, approved the design of the General Staff insignia to take effect 1 July 1904. The device has been in continual use since that date. The insignia was originally worn only by officers, in the grade of captain and above, detailed to the General Staff Corps. Authority for its wear was later extended to officers detailed to General Staff Corps with troops.

When the Department of the Army became the legal successor to the War Department, the word "Corps" in the title of branch officers detailed to the General Staff Corps was dropped. The device is now worn by officers detailed in orders to the Army General Staff and to General Staff with troops.

The star is symbolic of the highest level in the Army and the Arms of the United States allude to the mission of the General Staff which is to exercise General Staff supervision over the management of the land forces of the United States.

Branch Colors: No color assigned.

⭐ Infantry

Infantry Branch: The Infantry is the main land combat force of the Military. In combat, the role of the infantry is to capture or destroy enemy ground forces and repel enemy attacks. Members of the Infantry are ground troops that engage with the enemy in close-range combat. Infantry has been the "Queen of Battle" since the days of the Romans.

Branch Insignia: Two gold color crossed vintage 1795 Springfield muskets, 3/4 inch in height.

Crossed muskets were first introduced into the Army as the insignia of officers and enlisted men of the Infantry effective 1 June 1876. In 1924 the branch insignia was standardized by the adoption of crossed 1795 model Springfield Arsenal muskets. This was the first official United States shoulder arm made in a government arsenal with interchangeable parts, caliber .69, flint lock, smooth bore, muzzle loader. The device adopted in 1922 has been in continual use since 1924. There have been slight modifications in the size of the insignia over the years; however, the basic design has remained unchanged.

Regimental Insignia: Personnel assigned to the Infantry branch affiliate with a specific regiment and wear the insignia of the affiliated regiment.

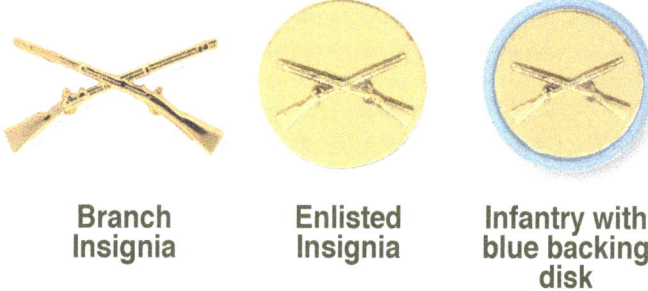

Branch Insignia | Enlisted Insignia | Infantry with blue backing disk

Regimental Coat of Arms: There is no standard infantry regimental flag to represent all of the Infantry regiments. Each regiment of Infantry has its own coat of arms which appears on the breast of a displayed eagle. The background of all the Infantry regimental flags is flag blue with yellow fringe.

Branch Colors: The Infantry color is light blue; however, Infantry regimental flags and guidons have been National Flag blue since 1835. White is used as a secondary color on the guidons for letters, numbers and insignia.

Birthday: 14 June 1775. The Infantry is the oldest branch in the Army. Ten companies of riflemen were authorized by the Continental Congress Resolve of 14 June 1775.

Infantry Blue Shoulder Cord

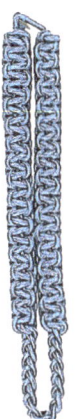

Infantry Blue Shoulder Cord
Officers and enlisted men of the Infantry who have been awarded the Combat Infantryman Badge or Expert Infantryman Badge or have completed the basic infantry training courses wear the infantry blue shoulder cord on the right shoulder of the Army dress and full dress uniform. The cord goes under the arm and attaches to a regulation small U.S. Army button attached to the shoulder seam 1/2 inch outside the right collar edge.

Infantry Hat Insignia Trim

Inspector General

Branch Insignia

Enlisted Insignia

Branch Insignia: A sword and fasces 3/4 inch in height, crossed and wreathed in gold color metal with the inscription "DROIT ET AVANT" *(Right and Forward)* in blue enamel on the upper part of the wreath.

On 26 February 1890, the Inspector General's insignia was approved by the Secretary of War. It consists of a crossed sword and fasces with wreath. The fasces, composed of an axe in a bundle of rods, was a symbol of authority of Roman magistrates.

Branch Colors: Dark Blue piped with light blue. The Inspector General's Department in 1851 had pompons of buff with upper one third in scarlet. In 1915, specifications established the facings as dark blue. The 14 October 1921 regulation established the colors as dark blue piped with white. Circular #70, dated 18 October 1936, announced the exchange of colors with the Judge Advocate General's Department that resulted in the present colors.

Judge Advocate General's Corps

Judge Advocate General's Corps: The Judge Advocate General's Corps is a special branch of the Army whose officers are all lawyers. Their duties include all areas of legal practice including criminal law, administrative and civil law, contract law, and international law.

Branch Insignia

Enlisted Insignia

Branch Insignia: A gold color sword and pen crossed and superimposed on a laurel wreath 11/16 inches in height.

In May 1890, *"a sword and pen crossed and wreathed embroidered in silver"* was originally adopted for wear by officers of the Judge Advocate General's Department. In 1899, the color was changed to gold. The pen represents the recording of testimony and the sword symbolizes the military character of the Corps. The wreath is symbolic of honor. The enlisted branch of service insignia was authorized on 4 August 1967.

Branch colors: Dark blue piped with white.

Birthday: 29 July 1775. The Office of Judge Advocate of the Army is deemed to have been created on 29 July 1775.

Army Medical Department

Medical Corps | Dental Corps | Veterinary Corps | Nurse Corps | Specialist Corps | Medical Service Corps | Enlisted Insignia

Medical Corps (MC) of the U.S. Army is a staff corps (non-combat specialty branch) of the Army Medical Department (AMEDD) consisting of commissioned medical officers – physicians with either an M.D. or a D.O. degree, at least one year of post-graduate clinical training, and a state medical license. During the Vietnam era, serious physician shortfalls were experienced by the Defense Department and osteopathic physicians, who had previously been excluded from active military service, were first admitted to the MC. To avoid reinstating another "doctor draft", the US Congress took steps to encourage medical students to enter the military as physicians. Completing this trend, medical school training has been provided for military students by the Uniformed Services University of the Health Sciences (USUHS) established in 1972.

The Dental Corps is a special branch of the Army. The Corps consists of commissioned officers who are Doctors of dental surgery or dental medicine. Their mission is to conserve the fighting strength by preserving oral health, treating oral disease, and supporting the combat medical mission.

The Veterinary Corps is a part of the Army Medical Department and is a special branch of the Army. The Corps directs its activities toward four areas: veterinary food inspection and hygiene, animal medical care, veterinary preventive medicine, and research and development.

Army Nurse Corps (AN or ANC) The ANC is the nursing service for the Army. The ANC is composed entirely of Registered Nurses (RNs). The Army Nurse Corps stopped being all-female in 1955. During the Vietnam War many Army Nurses saw deployment to South East Asia. Army Nurses staffed all major Army hospitals in the theatre, including: Cam Ranh Bay, Da Nang, and Saigon. Vietnam would be the first major deployment of men as nurses into the combat theater, as men could be located in more hazardous locations than what was considered safe for females. Many Army Nurses faced enemy fire for the first time due to the unconventional nature of the conflict, and several Nurses died from direct enemy fire. On at least one occasion the US Army hospital at Cam Ranh Bay was assaulted and severely damaged, with a loss of both patient and staff life.

Army Medical Specialist Corps: The Army Medical Specialist Corps is a part of the Army Medical Department and is a special branch of the Army. The Nutrition Care Section, Physical Therapist Section, and the Occupational Therapist Section make up the Medical Specialist Corps.

The Medical Service Corps is a special branch of the Army Medical Department. The focus of the Medical Service Corps is on matters such as logistics and supply, support, and administration, and the provision of services like lab testing, pharmacy, and environmental science, and of medical specialties such as psychology and optometry.

Branch Insignia: A gold color medal caduceus, 1 inch in height. *(With the exception of the basic Medical Corps, each Corps is identified by black enamel letters centered on the caduceus indicative of their Corps.)* The insignia for Medical Service Corps is silver. Rooted in mythology, the caduceus, historically an emblem of physicians, symbolizes knowledge, wisdom, promptness and various aspects of medical skill.

Branch Colors: Maroon piped with white.

Birthday: 27 July 1775. On 4 June 1968, the Army Medical Service was redesignated the Army Medical Department.

⭐ Military Intelligence

Military Intelligence encompasses integration of all Military Intelligence functions at both the tactical and strategic levels. They plan, conduct, and supervise intelligence collection resources, analysis of the resultant raw intelligence information, and the production and dissemination of finished all-source intelligence in the form of briefings and written reports to the commander.

Branch Insignia   **Enlisted Insignia**   **Regimental Coat of Arms**

Historically, intelligence always has been an essential element of Army operations during war as well as during so-called periods of peace. In the past, requirements were met by personnel from the Army Intelligence and Army Security Reserve branches. To meet the Army's increased requirements for national and tactical intelligence, an Intelligence and Security Branch was established in the Army effective 1 July 1962 by GO 38, 3 July 1962. On 1 July 1967, the branch was redesignated as Military Intelligence.

Branch Insignia: On a gold color metal dagger, point up, 1 1/4 inches overall in height, a gold color metal heraldic sun composed of four straight and four wavy alternating rays surmounted by a gold heraldic rose, the petals dark blue enamel.

The insignia was originally approved in 1962 for the Army Intelligence and Security Branch and redesignated to the Military Intelligence Branch on 1 July 1967. The sun, composed of four straight and four wavy alternating rays, is the symbol of Helios who, as God of the Sun, could see and hear everything. The four straight rays of the sun symbol also allude to the four points of the compass and the worldwide mission of the Military Intelligence Branch. The placement of the sun symbol beneath the rose *(an ancient symbol of secrecy)* refers to the operations and activities being conducted under circumstances forbidding disclosure. The partially concealed unsheathed dagger alludes to the aggressive and protective requirements and the element of physical danger inherent in the mission. The color gold signifies successful accomplishment and the dark blue signifies vigilance and loyalty.

Branch Colors: Oriental blue piped with silver gray.

Birthday: 1 July 1962.

Medals of America Press 19

⭐ Military Police Corps

Military Police Corps: The Military Police Corps provides Military Police (MP) support to combat operations, law enforcement, security of U.S. Government resources, criminal investigation, and corrections. The combat support role provides the tactical commander with a force that is highly organized, trained, and responsive to the battlefield commander.

Branch Insignia: Two crossed gold color metal pistols 3/4 inch in height.

The insignia was approved in 1922. The old type pistol sometimes referred to as the Harper's Ferry Pistol *(made at the Harper's Ferry Arsenal)*, was selected since it is the first American Military pistol and remained the Army model for

Branch Insignia   **Enlisted Insignia**

many years. The parts of this weapon were standardized and interchangeable, thereby marking an advance in arms.

Branch Colors: Green piped with yellow.

Birthday: 26 September 1941. The Provost Marshal General's Office and Corps of Military Police were established in 1941. Although a "Provost Marshal" can be found as early as January 1776, and a Provost Corps as early as 1778.

⭐ National Guard Bureau

Branch Insignia: Two crossed gold color metal fasces superimposed on an eagle displayed with wings reversed, 1 inch in height.

On 12 July 1920, the Commission of Fine Arts was requested by the War Department to render assistance in the design of an insignia for the Militia Bureau. The citizen-soldier is represented by the fasces, denoting the unity of the States, and the eagle represented the Federal Government. The original design and model were made by Anthony de Francisci, the Sculptor, and were approved by the Commission. In a memorandum from the Chief of

Staff to the Quartermaster General, under date of 12 May 1921, the design and model submitted by the Commission of Fine Arts, was approved. The symbolism of the design, as expressed by the Commission of Fine Arts, was adopted and has remained the basic symbolism since 12 May 1921.

The **Militia Bureau** was redesignated as the National Guard Bureau on 15 June 1933, in accordance with Public Law No. 64, 73d Congress, and the name of the branch insignia was changed accordingly.

Branch Colors: Dark Blue.

⭐ Ordnance Corps

Ordnance Corps: The Ordnance Corps develops, produces, acquires, and support weapons systems, ammunition, missiles and ground mobility material during peace and war in order to provide combat power for the Army. The Ordnance Branch encompasses all functions related to the life cycle management of its three commodities: tank/automotive materiel, munitions materiel, and missile materiel.

Branch Insignia   **Enlisted Insignia**

Branch Insignia: A gold color metal shell and flame 1 inch in height.

The use of the "shell and flame" by the Ordnance Corps dates back to 1832; it is considered to be the oldest branch insignia of the Army. Similar insignia had been used by the British Army. After its adoption by the American Army, the design was used by the Artillery as well as the Ordnance until 1834 when the crossed cannon was adopted by the Artillery. In 1835, the shell and flame was used on a button for members of the Ordnance Corps and the design had been used in various items worn on the uniform since it was first adopted.

Branch Colors: Crimson piped with yellow.

Birthday: 14 May 1812. The Ordnance Department was established by the act of 14 May 1812.

⭐ Quartermaster Corps

Quartermaster Corps: The Quartermaster Corps plans and directs the activities of Army units and organizations engaged in the acquisition, receipt, storage, preservation, and issue of equipment, repair parts, fortification/construction material, subsistence, petroleum products, water, and other general supplies.

Branch Insignia   **Enlisted Insignia**

Branch Insignia: A gold color eagle with wings spread perched on a wheel with a blue felloe set with thirteen gold stars, having thirteen gold spokes and the hub white with a red center; superimposed on the wheel a gold sword and key crossed diagonally hilt and bow up. The insignia is 3/4 inches in height.

The insignia of the Quartermaster Department was approved in 1895. The design was retained when the Corps was established in 1912. After World War I, the earlier design, with the eagle's head superimposed on one wing, was changed to depict the head above the wings. The wagon wheel is symbolic of transportation and symbolizes the original colonies and the origin of the Corps during the Revolutionary War. The sword, indicative of the military forces, and the key, alluding to storekeeping functions, symbolizes the control of military supplies by the Quartermaster Corps. The eagle symbolizes our nation; red, white, and blue are the national colors.

Branch Colors: Buff - In 1884, the color buff was adopted which is presently used. Light blue is still used as the secondary color on flags for Quartermaster units.

Birthday: 16 June 1775. The Quartermaster Corps, originally designated the Quartermaster Department, was established on 16 June 1775.

⭐ Signal Corps

Signal Corps: Plans and manage information systems and communications that support the command and control of the Army's forces. Signal personnel direct and control the installation, operations, maintenance, and reconfiguration of networks of information systems for theater/tactical, strategic, and sustaining base operations and the operation of the Army portion of the global defense communications systems.

Branch Insignia: Two signal flags crossed, dexter flag white with a red center, the sinister flag red with a white center, staffs gold, with a flaming torch of gold color metal upright at center of crossed flags; 7/8 inch in height.

Branch Insignia

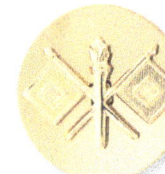
Enlisted Insignia

"Crossed flags" have been used by the Signal Corps since 1868, when they were prescribed for wear on the uniform coat by enlisted men of the Signal Corps. In 1884, a burning torch was added to the insignia and the present design adopted on 1 July 1884. The flags and torch are symbolic of signaling or communication.

Branch Colors: Orange piped with white.

Birthday: 21 June 1860. The Signal Corps was authorized as a separate branch of the Army by act of Congress on 3 March 1863.

However, the Signal Corps dates its existence from 21 June 1860 when Congress authorized the appointment of one signal officer in the Army, and a War Department order carried the following assignment: "Signal Department - Assistant Surgeon Albert J. Myer to be Signal Officer, with the rank of Major, June 17, 1860, to fill an original vacancy."

⭐ Staff Specialist, ARNG/USAR, Officers

Branch Insignia: A sword 1 3/8 inches in length laid horizontally across the upper part of an open book. Below the sword and across the lower corners of the book, two laurel branches crossed at the stems. Insignia 13/16 inch in height of gold color metal.

Prior to World War II, all officers were assigned to one of the arms or services and had an appropriate branch of service insignia. In November 1941, an insignia was created which consisted of the Coat of Arms of the United States within a ring, for officers who were not members of, or on duty with an arm or service, and the Specialist Reserve. Following World War II, unassigned officers became a part of the Staff and Administrative Reserve Section in the Army National Guard and Organized Reserve Corps.

The Insignia was designed by the Heraldic Section, Office of The Quartermaster General and approved 5 February 1948. On 23 September 1949, the Staff and Administrative Reserve branch insignia was redesignated for the Staff Specialist Reserve branch insignia. The Staff Specialist is still a branch of the U.S. Army Reserve *(formerly the Organized Reserve Corps)* but has no equivalent in the Regular Army. The book represents regulations, while the laurel sprays symbolize the honors received in the administration of military regulations. The sword represents the military nature of the regulations.

Branch Color: Green

⭐ Transportation Corps

Transportation Corps: The Transportation Corps is a combat service support branch of the Army. It is responsible for the movement of personnel and material by truck, rail, air, and sea. It is one of three U.S. Army logistics branches, the others being the Quartermaster Corps and the Ordnance Corps.

The Transportation Corps helicopters companies were the first intact American Army units to arrive in Vietnam during the Advisory phase in 1962, and the Transportation Corps also was part of the logistical footprint at the subordinate ports in order to bring in the combat divisions in 1965.

Branch Insignia

Enlisted Insignia

Branch Insignia: A ship's steering wheel, superimposed thereon a shield charged with a winged car wheel on a rail, all of gold color metal, 1 inch in height.

In 1919, "a winged car wheel, flanged, on a rail, surrounded by a rim one inch in diameter" was approved as the insignia of the Transportation Corps. The Army Reorganization Act, 4 June 1920, placed all transportation except military railways under the Quartermaster General. The Transportation Corps essentially in its present form was organized on 31 July 1942 as a result of the Army reorganization of 1942 and has functioned since then as one of the services. The present Transportation Corps insignia is based on that of the World War I Corps, with shield and ship's wheel added. The winged car wheel is for rail transportation and the Mariner's helm for transport by water. The U.S. highway marker shield is for land transportation.

Branch Colors: Brick red piped with golden yellow. When the Transportation Corps was established in 1942, the brick red piped with golden yellow was assigned as the branch color.

Birthday: 31 July 1942. The historical background of the Transportation Corps starts with World War I. Prior to that time, transportation operations were chiefly the responsibility of the Quartermaster General.

⭐ Warrant Officer Branch *(Obsolete 9 July 2004)*

Branch Insignia: A distinctive insignia was approved for warrant officers on 12 May 1921 and removed 9 July 2004. It consisted of an eagle rising with wings displayed, adapted from the great seal of the United States.

The National eagle is standing on two arrows which symbolize the military arts and sciences. The rising eagle is enclosed within a wreath. Warrant Officers now wear the basic branch insignia and colors based on their primary MOS. Warrant Officer's replaced their "Eagle Rising" hat insignia with the "Coat of Arms of the United States" insignia on their service caps effective 9 July 2004.

Branch Colors: The Army Warrant Officer Corps color was brown. The color emanated from the brown strands from burlap bags used by the Mine Planter Service. Now Warrant Officers wear the basic branch color of their primary MOS.

Warrant Officer Corps: A warrant officer is an officer appointed by warrant by the Secretary of the Army, based on technical and tactical competence. They are highly specialized experts who, operate, maintain, administer and manage the Army's equipment, support activities or technical systems for an entire career. Warrant Officers work in every branch of service as reflected by the needs of the Army. Warrant officers specifically trained as pilots or as other specialists and spend their entire career in the Aviation or other branches. As of 9 July 2004 they wear the insignia of the branch they are serving in.

⭐ Rank Insignia, Combat, Skill and Identification Badges During Vietnam

Using the Army Class A Green Uniform it is easier to start with an overview of both the enlisted and officers uniform to understand the location of rank /grade insignia , branch of service, shoulder sleeve insignia, combat , skill and identification badges as well as ribbons and unit awards. Basically the only two difference between officers and enlisted uniforms was that officers wore their rank on their shoulder and enlisted personel wore their rank on their sleeves. The other difference was officers wore a U.S. and their branch insignia on each lapel while enlisted personnel worn a disk with a US on their left lapel and a disk with their branch on their right lapel.

Wear of awards and insignia on the Army Class A green uniform for officer personnel during the Vietnam War.

The diagram below details the location and wear of awards and insignia on the Army Class A green uniform for enlisted personnel during the Vietnam War.

24 Insignia, Rank and Badges, U.S. Army Vietnam

Background and Development of Enlisted Ranks

In January 1942, during World War II, the grades of technician in the third, fourth and fifth grades were added. A letter "T" was added just under the chevrons for grades three, four and five.

The first sergeant was designated first grade from the second grade in 1942, changing to three chevrons and arc of three bars, and a hollow lozenge in the center. This change also included the material as khaki chevrons, arcs, T's and lozenge on dark blue cotton background or olive-drab wool chevrons, arcs, T's and lozenge on a dark blue wool background.

In 1948, sergeant 4th grade was discontinued and recruit was added as the 7th grade. The new insignia was smaller and the colors changed with combat personnel wearing gold color background with dark blue chevrons, arcs and lozenges. Noncombatant personnel wore dark blue with gold color chevrons, arcs, and lozenge. Technicians were also deleted from the rank structure.

The size of the chevrons was changed from 2 inches wide to 3 1/8 inches wide for male personnel in 1951 and pay grades reversed with master sergeant becoming E7. The insignia continued to remain two inches wide for female personnel. The insignia was authorized to be manufactured in one color: a dark blue background with olive-drab chevrons, arcs, and lozenges.

In 1955, after the Korean War, new rank titles were authorized: Master Sergeant E-7 (1st Sgt. was an occupational title) & Master Specialist, Sergeant 1st Class, Specialist 1st Class E-6, Sergeant, Specialist 2d Class E5, Corporal, Specialist 3d Class E-4, Private First Class E-3, Private E2, E-2, Private E1, E-1.

The rank insignia background color changed in 1956 to Army Green (the new uniform color) or Army Blue with the gold chevrons, arc, lozenge and eagle. The new specialists insignia had an embroidered eagle device on a two inch wide arched background with chevrons on top of the eagle.

The specialist insignia was part of an effort to differentiate between the Army's technical or support specialists who were not NCOs and the NCOs. Grades E-8 and E9 were added in June 1958. The specialist insignia was enlarged for males and remained the same size for female personnel. The new insignia were:

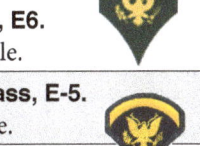

Master Specialist, E7. Three arcs above the eagle.	
Specialist First Class, E6. Two arcs above the eagle.	
Specialist Second Class, E-5. One arc above the eagle.	
Specialist Third Class, E4. Eagle device only.	

Sergeant Major, E9. Three chevrons above three arcs with a five pointed star in the center.	
Specialist Nine, E9. Three arcs above the eagle and two chevrons below.	
First Sergeant, E8. Three chevrons above three arcs with a lozenge in the center.	

For morale purposes, the old chevrons and titles for E5, E6 and E7 were authorized for wear until the individual was promoted or demoted.

Master Sergeant, E8. Three chevrons above three arcs.	
Specialist Eight, E8. Three arcs above the eagle and one chevron below.	
Platoon Sergeant or Sergeant first class, E7. Three chevrons above two arcs.	
Specialist Seven, E7. Three arcs above the eagle device.	
Staff Sergeant, E6. Three chevrons above one arc.	
Specialist Six, E6. Two arcs above the eagle device.	
Sergeant, E5. Three chevrons.	
Specialist Five, E5. One arc above the eagle device.	
Corporal, E4. Two chevrons.	
Specialist Four, E4. Eagle device only.	
Private First Class. One chevron.	

Specialist Eight and Specialist Nine grades were discontinued in 1965. Subdued black metal insignia was authorized for wear on the collar of the work uniforms in 1967.

1968 saw the Command Sergeant Major insignia authorized, changing the large star in the center to a smaller star with a wreath around the star. The single chevron previously authorized for private first class, was authorized for private E2 while a new insignia of one chevron above and one arc below was authorized for private first class.

Shiny brass metal insignia was authorized for wear on the overcoat, raincoat and windbreaker in 1975. Specialist Seven was discontinued in 1978. A Sergeant Major of the Army insignia of three chevrons above three arcs with two stars centered was established in 1979.

The grades Specialist Five and Specialist Six were discontinued in October 1985. Sergeant Major of the Army insignia changed in 1994 adding the United States coat of arms between the two stars in the center. The male and female sizes of chevrons were changed to large and small insignia in 1996.

Army Enlisted Rank Insignia during the Vietnam War

Description	Rank	May 1968-79
Sergeant Major/E-9 (SGM): The senior NCO rank. Specialist E9 was dropped in 1965. Since 1968, the senior SGM for a Battalion or higher is designated as a Command Sergeant Major (CSM). In 1966, the rank of Sergeant Major of the Army was established, considered a higher grade than sergeant major or command sergeant major from 1968), the Sergeant Major of the Army first rank insignia in 1979 had two stars in the center.	E-9	SMA CSM SGM
First Sergeant/E-8 (1SG): Senior Noncommissioned officer in charge of an entire Company, Battery or Troop. Works directly for the commander in the care and administration of the company soldiers. **Master Sergeant/E-8 (MSG):** Same pay grade as First Sergeant, but less responsibility. May be in charge of more than one platoon/section. Can be acting First Sergeant. Specialist E8 (SP8) was dropped in 1965.	E-8	1SG MSG SP8
Platoon Sergeant/Sergeant First Class/E-7(SFC): The first of the senior enlisted ranks, usually in charge of a platoon/section. Can be an acting First Sergeant. **Specialist E7** (SP7) was dropped in 1978	E-7	SFC SP7
Staff Sergeant/E-6 (SSgt.): Given more responsibility than sergeant. Can be given charge of a platoon/section, or administrative duties. Must be technically proficient in his job, an expert. **Specialist E6** (SP6) was dropped in 1985.	E-6	SSG SP6
Sergeant/E-5 (Sgt.): Takes responsibility in day to day care of soldiers, training, and discipline. Normally serves three years before considered for promotion, but can be considered early with a waiver, or recommendation. Accrues points for promotion by going to college, taking correspondence courses, military schools, and awards and accommodations. Accrual of points begins at Private/E-1. **Specialist E5** (SP5) was dropped in 1985.	E-5	SGT SP5
Corporal/E-4 (CPL.): First Non-Commissioned Officer rank, has responsibility for lower enlisted. Can be put in charge of other enlisted men of lower rank. Must serve two years and go to Primary Leadership Development Course school to get this promotion. **Specialist/E-4 (Spc.):** Same pay grade as Corporal, but no command responsibility. Does not have to go to Primary Leadership Development Course school to get this promotion.	E-4	CPL SPC
Private first class/E-3 (PFC): Addressed as Private. E-2 can be promoted to E-3 after one year, earlier upon request by a supervisor.	E-3	PFC
Private/E-2 (Pvt2): Same name, but one pay grade up. E-1 is promoted to E-2 automatically after 1 year if there is no negative conduct. Insignia: 1 chevron on each collar of a shirt or uniform sleeve.	E-2	Private

26 Insignia, Rank and Badges, U.S. Army Vietnam

US Army Enlisted Rank Insignia

1965 Dress & Combat	1959
SGM	Sergeant Major / Specialist E9
1SG / MSG	1SG / MSG / SP8
SFC / SP7	SFC / SP7
SSG / SP6	SSG / SP6
SGT / SP5	SGT / SP5
CPL / SPC	CPL / SPC
PFC	PFC
Private	None

Officer & Warrant Officer Candidate School Insignia

OCS Old Shoulder Insignia

OCS Current Shoulder Insignia

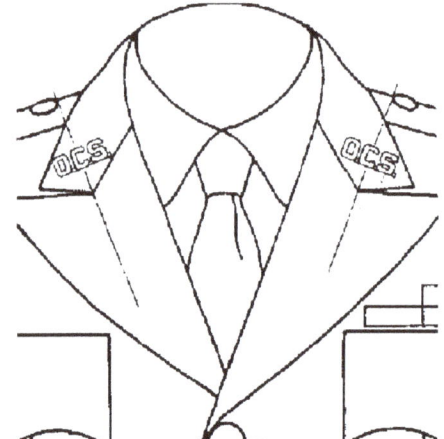

OCS Collar Insignia

Warrant Officer Candidate Collar Insignia

Officer Candidate School (*OCS*) and Warrant Officer Candidate School are schools for enlisted personnel to qualify for appointment as Commissioned Officers or Warrant Officers in the United States Army Reserve for both Active Army and Reserve service. The OCS and WOC insignia is worn in place of the U.S. insignia on the class A uniform lapels or on the shirt collar.

Warrant Officer's Insignia of Rank

The warrant officer rank was created to fill special positions requiring greater technical skill and responsibility than a noncommissioned officer but without the responsibility of command. The military grade of warrant officer originated several hundred years ago during the early period of the British Navy. The less experienced officers of the Royal Navy relied heavily on the technical expertise, knowledge, and allegiance of senior sailors who were rewarded with a Royal Warrant. The Royal Warrant designation clearly distinguished them from the other sailors while maintaining the strict class system of the period.

In September, 1956, with the other Military Services concurrence, four new warrant officer insignia were approved for use across the services. The only differences were that each service used its own unique color on the bar. The first two grades in the Army were gold and brown while the two senior grades were silver and brown.

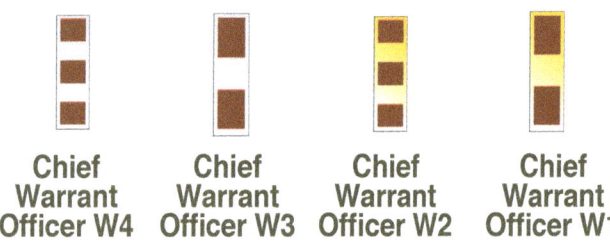

New, easier to identify insignia were approved in June, 1970 for wear as of July 1, 1972. Based on the anticipated addition of two warrant grades, new insignia for W5 and W6 were developed but never authorized for wear.

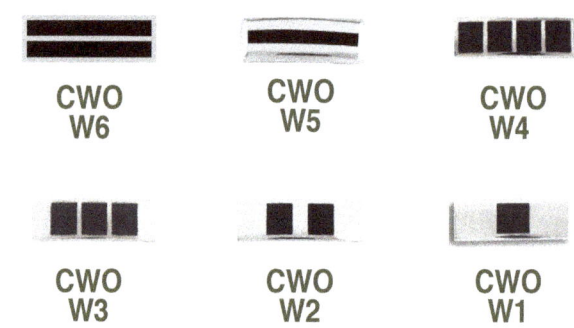

The Chief of Staff approved Master Warrant Officer (W4) insignia on April 8, 1988 designating certain CWO W4 as master warrants. Master Warrant Officer appointment required completion of the Warrant Officer school at Fort Rucker. The first class graduated on December 5, 1991, establishing the grade of CW5. On 9 July 2004, Master Warrant Officer W5 was approved for continued use.

U.S. Army Commissioned Rank Insignia

With the exception of the warrant officer grades, the present Army officer rank is the same design as used in World War II. The difference today is the adoption of slide-on soft cloth rank epaulets and a simplified mess dress rank design.

Second Lieutenant - One gold-colored bar of the same type as for a First Lieutenant 1 by 3/8 inch. Typically, the entry level commissioned officer rank. Second Lieutenants normally spend six months of their time in a training status, preparing for the first assignment in their specialty. Lieutenant comes from the French word lieu *(place)* tenant *(holding)*. An officer who acts in the place of another, the Lieutenant's duty is often to be his superior officer's deputy. By use, it has come to mean the officer who is a subordinate of a captain. This most junior officer rank was created in the British Navy in the 16th century to provide an officer ready and able to take command should the Captain be absent or unable to command.

First Lieutenant - One silver-colored bar of the same type as for a Captain. Increased responsibility assignments as Executive officers of a company and junior staff officers, are typical of this rank. In the 17th century, the Lieutenant rank in Great Britain was given to those noblemen in training to become Captains. The bar rank is 1inch by 3/8 inches in regular size.

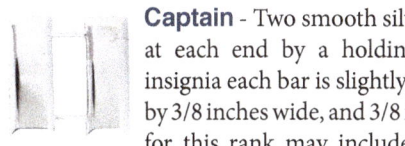

Captain - Two smooth silver-colored bars, attached at each end by a holding bar. For the shoulder insignia each bar is slightly curved, 1 1/8 inches long by 3/8 inches wide, and 3/8 inches apart. Assignments for this rank may include company commanders, branch chiefs, staff officers, and instructors. Captain comes from the Latin word "caput", meaning head and of the Latin word capitaneus *(chief)*. Although a Captain could be the head of any organization *(for example the Spanish; Captain General)*, the rank is associated with officers commanding a company, battery or troop.

Major - A seven-pointed, gold-colored oak leaf, raised and veined. Shoulder insignia; slightly curved, one inch from stem tip to center leaf tip. The term was taken from the Latin word meaning "greater." The rank initially evolved from the rank of Sergeant Major, which in the 16th century was just below Lieutenant Colonel. In succeeding centuries, the rank became "Major" as the "Sergeant" portion was dropped. Typical assignments are battalion executive officer or staff officer.

Lieutenant Colonel - A seven-pointed, silver-colored oak leaf, raised and veined. Shoulder insignia; slightly curved, one inch from stem tip to center leaf tip. Collar insignia; flat, 2 3/32 inches from stem tip to center leaf tip. Typical assignments are battalion commander or staff officer.

Colonel - A silver-colored spread eagle, made in pairs, right and left, talons of one foot grasping an olive branch, the other, a bundle of 13 arrows. Shoulder insignia; slightly curved, with 1 1/2 inch wing span. The term evolved in the 16th century from the Spanish King, Ferdinand, who called the commander of his columns "cabo de colunela" which later became colonel in the French and British armies. The current pronunciation of "kernel" was established by the British. *(Colonel may come from the Italian word colonello meaning little column, an officer commanding a 'column' of soldiers or may come from the word column, a column, or corona, a crown.)* The head of the eagle is worn facing forward.

Brigadier General - One silver-colored star, 1 inch in height. General originally meant to be of similar 'birth' or 'class' with the sovereign; the more recent use is to be familiar with all facets of the army, no longer a specialist in one area, and a "general officer". In summary, any officer in general command of all troops. Original General ranks were: Captain General, Lieutenant General, Sergeant Major General and Brigadier General *(A corporal in French is a Brigadier)*. This explains why a Lieutenant General out ranks a Major General. Major General was originally Sergeant Major General.

Major General - Two silver-colored stars of the same type and arranged in the same manner as for a Lieutenant General. A Major General normally commands a Division, large military post, a branch of the service *(i.e. Armor Branch)* or a high level staff branch.

Lieutenant General - Three silver-colored stars, of the same type and arranged in the same manner as for a General, except the distance between centers of adjacent shoulder stars is one inch. Normally commands a Corps or a major division of the Army staff.

General - Four silver-colored, five-pointed, pyramid-shaped stars. Shoulder stars are one inch in diameter and are either fastened together on a metal holding bar or placed individually with one point of each star in the same line; distance between the centers of adjacent stars is 3/4 inch. Normally, commands an Army, a major command of the Army, or serves as Chief of Staff or Vice Chief of Staff of the Army.

New style subdued pin on rank

Medals of America Press

Hat Badges, Buttons and Lapel Pins

Army Officer Hat Badge (Female)

Army Officer Hat Badge (Male)

Former Warrant Officer Hat Badge

Enlisted Female Hat Badge

Enlisted Hat Badge

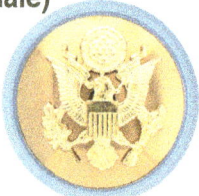

Infantry Hat Insignia Trim

Band Hat Badge

US Insignia Officer

Enlisted US Letters

Infantry US Insignia Trim

Current Army Uniform Button

Army Engineer Corps Officers Button

ROTC Insignia Cadet | Officer Candidate School Insignia | Warrant Officer Candidate Insignia

Aide Insignia

Although not considered a branch of service, U.S. Army officers assigned as aides to flag or equivalent grade officers replace their branch of service insignia for a special aide-de-camp insignia that denote the grade or position of the officer the aide supports. Because these collar insignia are branch immaterial, officers continue to wear their original branch of service colors

Aide to President

Aide to Vice President

Aide to Secretary of Defense

Aide to Secretary of the Army

Aide to Under Secretary of the Army

Aide to Chairman, Joint Chiefs of Staff

Aide to Vice Chairman, Joint Chiefs of Staff

Aide to Chief of Staff of the Army

Aide to Vice Chief of Staff of the Army

Aide to General of the Army

Aide to General

Aide to Lieutenant General

Aide to Major General

Aide to Brigadier General

Army Officers Hat Insignia

In 1895, the Army moved from branch insignia on the officers cap to the national eagle. The all gilt eagle, which is the coat of arms of the United States, became the official hat insignia for all officers in 1903. The glory with 13 stars is over the eagles head and the right claw offers an olive branch while the left grasps 13 arrows.

Army Female Officers Hat Insignia

In 1943, the Women's Army Auxiliary Corps became the Women's Army Corps and the Army replaced their "walking eagle" insignia with the same style hat insignia as male officers, the gold gilt national eagle. The women's officer hat insignia changed color in 1951 to an antique bronze when a new taupe uniform was introduced for the WAC. The introduction of the Army blue uniform and Army green uniform caused the hat insignia to return to its original gold color in 1964. The current female Army officer hat insignia is about 1 1/2 inches wide, slightly smaller than their male counterparts, but identical in every other aspect.

Army Warrant Officers Hat Insignia During Vietnam

(Current) Warrant Officers initially wore enlisted cap devices until 1921 when they wore a black metal eagle of the design created by the Fine Arts Commission. The insignia became obsolete in 2004. This insignia was also worn by Pilot Warrant Officers during World War II.

West Point Cadets Hat Insignia

(Current) United States military academy hat brass. The military hat insignia worn by West Point cadets is the coat of arms of the Military Academy. It has the shield the United States, bearing the helmet of Pallas over a Greek sword and surmounted by an eagle, displays a scroll with the motto, Duty, Honor, Country, West Point MDCCCV USMA, all in a gold color.

Reserve Officers Training Corps Hat and collar Insignia

While there are numerous variations of the Reserve Officer Training Corps hat brass, this is the most common. The ROTC initials are surrounded by a laurel wreath in a gilt color. The use of the national eagle with the letters ROTC is not authorized but is used by some schools.

Army Enlisted Hat Insignia

The Enlisted Hat Insignia was originally introduced in World War I. The insignia consist of a gold colored disk with the national coat of arms eagle mounted directly in the center. In 1952, a blue plastic disk, 1 3/4 inches wide was authorized to the worn by enlisted infantrymen to enhance their prestige and morale. Other branches have produced branch colored rims to go around their hat brass but all of these are non regulation. Only the infantry enlisted soldier is authorized to wear blue trim behind his hat insignia.

Army Female Enlisted Hat Insignia

Enlisted women's hat insignia consist of a gold colored circle with the national code of arms eagle mounted directly in the center. It is the same as enlisted men except the coat of arms of the United States Eagle rest in a gilt colored circle while the male insignia is mounted on a disk.

Army Bandsman's Hat Insignia

Army band member's hat brass approved in 1943 consisted of a gilt lyre, with the letters U.S. imposed on the lyre all of which was surrounded by a gilt wreath. A new design shown here was introduced in 1968 which is much more elaborate.

U.S. Letters for Officers and Enlisted

The letters U. S. are probably the oldest and most common United States Army markings going back to the original buttons used in the Revolution.

Current Army Uniform Button

The Army officer and enlisted buttons are gold plated with the Coat of Arms of the United States superimposed. Optional white gold anodized aluminum buttons worn during the Vietnam War are no longer authorized.

Army Engineer Corps Officers Button

The Corps of Engineers officer buttons are of a unique and distinct design not worn by the rest of the Army. The button consists of an Eagle holding the motto "Essayons" (*Let Us Try*) over a base surrounded by water and a rising sun. The design reflects early Corps of Engineers duties, which included the building of Harbor fortifications.

⭐ U.S. Army Badges and Tabs

Introduction to Badges

1782 Badge of Military Merit

The Army's purpose for awarding badges and tabs is for recognition of the high degree of skill, proficiency and excellence in test, competition and performance of duty. Although General Washington established the Badge of Military Merit, the Army was very slow to recognize the value of military badges as a matter of personal pride and public recognition for professional military skills.

By the early 1900s, Army regulations began to address the wear of badges but certainly not in the modern sense as we do now. Besides decorations and medals *(which were referred to then as badges)* the badges of military societies and of Civil War corps and division were authorized for wear on the uniform. The lack of official badges led the Army to accept badges to wear on the uniform from various military societies for men who in their own right or right of inheritance were members of the Army during the Revolution, War of 1812, Civil War, Spanish-American War etc. .

Military Aviator Badge (1913)

It was flying that led the way for the first of the skill badges when the Army authorized the first military aviator badge in the fall of 1913. World War I saw the first cloth badges for military aviators and observers. Badges followed for aviation mechanics and different types of pilots until the new Army Air Service had 13 different badges to reflect their skills.

Between World War I and II, badges for marksmanship began to finally appear as the Army realized the importance of recognizing key professional skills.

World War II saw the introduction of a comprehensive badge system to recognize skills and performance. Today, badges are divided into five types of badges:

(1) Combat and special skill badges which are awarded for proficiency in performance of duty under hazardous conditions and circumstances of extraordinary hardship as well as special qualifications and successful completion of prescribed course of training.

(2) Marksmanship badges and tabs which are awarded to indicate the degree in which an individual has qualified in prescribed weapons firing courses or events.

(3) Identification badges are authorized to be worn as public evidence of deserved honor and distinction and to denote service in specified assignments.

(4) Locally authorized special skill badge authority to Major Commanders was rescinded in September 1986. They are no longer allowed but were popular in Korea.

(5) Badges awarded by other U.S. Services and foreign governments which must be approved before wear.

The following pages show these badges in the order of precedence outlined in DA Pam 670-1.

Combat and Special Skill Badge Wear Today

Combat and special skill badges and tabs authorized for wear on the Army uniform are listed below in order of group precedence:

(1) **Group 1.** Combat Infantryman badges *(three awards)*; Expert Infantryman badge .

(2) **Group 2.** Combat Medical badges *(three awards)*; Expert Field Medical badge.

(3) **Group 3.** Army Aviator badges *(three degrees)*; Flight Surgeon badges (three degrees); Aviation badges *(three degrees)*; Explosive Ordnance Disposal badges *(three degrees)*.

(4) **Group 4.** Parachutist badges *(three degrees)*; Parachutist badges with combat jump device *(four degrees are shown)*; Pathfinder badge; Air Assault badge; Ranger and Special Forces tab metal replicas .

(5) **Group 5.** Diver badges *(six badges)*; Driver and Mechanic badge; Parachute Rigger badge.

(6) **Physical fitness badge.** The physical fitness badge is authorized for wear only on the physical fitness uniform and did become authorized after the Vietnam War.

Combat Infantryman Badges Group One

First Award

Second Award

Third Award

Fourth Award

I. **Description:** A silver and enamel badge 1 inch in height and 3 inches in width, consisting of an Infantry musket on a light blue bar with a silver border on and over an elliptical oak wreath. Stars are added at the top of the wreath to indicate subsequent awards; one star for the second award, two stars for the third award and three stars for the fourth award.

II. **Symbolism:** The bar is blue, the color associated with the Infantry branch. The musket is adapted from the Infantry insignia of branch and represents the first official U.S. shoulder arm, the 1795 model Springfield Arsenal musket. It was adopted as the official Infantry branch insignia in 1924. The oak wreath symbolizes steadfastness, strength and loyalty.

III. **Award Eligibility:** Awarded to personnel in the grade of Colonel or below with an Infantry military occupational specialty who have satisfactorily performed duty while assigned as a member of an Infantry unit, brigade or smaller size, after 6 December 1941, when engaged in active ground combat. Expanded to permit award to Command Sergeants Major of Infantry battalions or brigades, effective 1 January 1967. Specific criteria for each conflict was also established. Only one award is authorized for service in Vietnam, Laos, Dominican Republic, Korea *(subsequent to 27 July 1954)*, Grenada, Panama, and Southwest Asia. The complete criteria for each area and inclusive dates are listed in Army Regulation 600-8-22.

IV. **Date Approved:** The Combat Infantryman Badge *(CIB)* was approved by the Secretary of War on 7 October 1943, and was initially referred to as the Combat Assault Badge; however, the name was changed to the Combat Infantryman Badge as announced in War Department Circular 269 dated 27 October 1943. On 8 February 1952, the Chief of Staff, Army, approved a proposal to add stars to the Combat Infantryman Badge to indicate award of the badge in separate wars. Under this change in policy, the badge was no longer limited to a one-time award, but may now be awarded to eligible individuals for each war in which they participated.

V. **Subdued Badges:** Subdued badges are authorized in metal and cloth. The metal badge has a black finish. The cloth badge has a base cloth with the rifle, wreath, stars and border of the bar embroidered in black.

 VI. **Miniature Badges:** A dress miniature badge, 1-1/4 inches in length is authorized for wear on the mess uniforms. A miniature badge, 1 3/4 inches is also authorized in lieu of the regular size badge.

⭐ Expert Infantryman Badge, Group One

I. **Description:** A silver and enamel badge 7/16 inch in height and 3 inches in width, consisting of an Infantry musket on a light blue bar with a silver border.

II. **Symbolism:** The bar is blue, the color associated with the Infantry branch. The musket is adapted from the Infantry insignia of branch and represents the first official U.S. shoulder arm, 1795 model Springfield Arsenal musket. It was adopted as the official Infantry branch insignia in 1924.

III. **Award Eligibility:** Personnel must meet Department of the Army established testing requirements and must possess a military occupational specialty within Career Management Field 11 (Infantry).

IV. **Date Approved:** The Expert Infantryman Badge was approved by the Secretary of War on 7 October 1943, and announced in War Department Circular 269 dated 27 October 1943.

V. **Subdued Badge:** The subdued badge is authorized in metal and cloth. The metal badge has a black finish. The cloth badge has a base cloth with the rifle and border of the bar embroidered in black.

VI. **Miniature Badge:** A miniature badge, 1 3/4 inches in length and 3/8 inch in height, is authorized in lieu of the regular size badge. A dress miniature badge, 1 1/4 inches in length and 3/16 inch in height is also authorized.

⭐ Combat Medical Badges, Group Two

First Award   **Second Award**   **Third Award**   **Fourth Award**

I. **Description:** An oxidized silver badge 1 inch in height and 1 1/2 inches in width, consisting of a stretcher crossed by a caduceus surmounted at top by a Greek cross, all on and over an elliptical oak wreath. Stars are added to indicate subsequent awards; one star at top for the second award, one star at top and one at bottom for the third award, one star at top and one at each side for the fourth award.

II. **Symbolism:** The Medical Corps insignia of branch, modified by the addition of a Greek cross suggesting the Geneva Convention between the wings and the entwined serpents, signifies the recipient's skills and expertise. It is superimposed upon a stretcher alluding to medical field service. The oak wreath symbolizes steadfastness, strength and loyalty.

III. **Award Eligibility:** Awarded to members of the Army Medical Department, Naval Medical Department or Air Force Medical Service who are in the grade of Colonel or below while assigned or attached to a medical unit of company or smaller size organic to an infantry unit during any period the infantry unit was engaged in active ground combat subsequent to 6 December 1941. Only one award is authorized for service in Vietnam, Laos, the Dominican Republic, Korea *(subsequent to 27 July 1954)*, Grenada, Panama, and Southwest Asia, regardless of whether an individual has served in one or more of these areas. Specific eligibility requirements by geographic area are listed in Army Regulation 600-8-22.

IV. **Date Approved:** The Combat Medical Badge was approved on 29 January 1945. In February 1951, the proposal to designate the badge as a one-time award was rescinded and it was approved for subsequent award during specified periods. The addition of stars to indicate subsequent awards was also approved.

V **Subdued Badges:** Subdued badges are authorized in metal and cloth. The metal badge is black. The cloth badge has a base cloth with the stretcher, caduceus, cross, wreath and stars embroidered in black.

VI. **Miniature Badges:** A dress miniature badge, 19/32 inch in height is authorized.

VII. **Remarks:** The CMB is authorized for award for the following qualifying wars, conflicts, and operations:

1. World War II *(7 December 1941 to 3 September 1945)*.
2. The Korean War *(27 June 1950 to 27 July 1953)*.
3. Republic of Vietnam Conflict *(2 March 1961 to 28 March 1973), combined with qualifying service in Laos (19 April 1961 to 6 October 1962)*.
4. Dominican Republic *(28 April 1965 to 1 September 1966)*.
5. Korea on the DMZ *(4 January 1969 to 31 March 1994)*.
6. El Salvador *(1 January 1981 to 1 February 1992)*.
7. Grenada *(23 October to 21 November 1983)*.
8. Joint Security Area, Panmunjom, Korea *(23 November 1984)*.
9. Panama *(20 December 1989 to 31 January 1990)*.
10. Southwest Asia Conflict *(17 January to 11 April 1991)*.
11. Somalia *(5 June 1992 to 31 March 1994)*.
12. Afghanistan *(Operation Enduring Freedom, 5 December 2001 to 20 August 2021)*
13. Iraq *(Operation Iraqi Freedom, 19 March 2003 to 15 Dec. 2011)*.

Expert Field Medical Badge, Group Two

I. **Description:** An oxidized silver badge 15/16 inch in height and 1-7/16 inches in width consisting of a stretcher crossed by a caduceus surmounted at top by a Greek cross.

II. **Symbolism:** The Medical Corps insignia of branch, modified by the addition of a Greek cross suggesting the Geneva Convention between the wings and the entwined serpents, signifies the recipient's skills and expertise. It is superimposed upon a stretcher alluding to medical field service.

III **Award Eligibility:** This badge recognizes Army personnel for attaining a high state of technical skill in field medical functions. It is awarded on the basis of proven skill and performance. Prior to being awarded the badge, personnel must successfully pass all test parts prescribed by Army Regulations.

IV. **Date Approved:** The Expert Medical Badge was approved on 18 June 1965.

V. **Subdued Badges:** Subdued badges are authorized in metal and cloth. The metal badge is black. The cloth badge has a base cloth with the stretcher, caduceus and cross embroidered in black.

VI. **Miniature Badges:** A dress miniature badge 9/16 inch in height is authorized.

Army Aviator Badges, Group Three

Army Aviator

Senior Army Aviator

Master Aviator

I. **Description:** An oxidized silver badge 3/4 inch in height and 2-1/2 inches in width, consisting of the shield of the coat of arms of the United States, on and over, a pair of displayed wings. A star is added above the shield to indicate qualification as a Senior Army Aviator. The star is surrounded with a laurel wreath to indicate qualification as a Master Army Aviator.

appropriate orders. Senior Army Aviator: Have 1,500 flying hours in aircraft or seven years from basic rating date. Master Army Aviator: Have 3,000 hours in aircraft or 15 years from basic rating date.

IV. **Date Approved:** The Aviator and Senior Aviator Badges were approved on 27 July 1950, and the Master Aviator Badge was approved on 12 February 1957.

Subdued Badge

Plated Badge

Silver Badge

II. **Symbolism:** The wings suggest flight and reflect the skills associated with aerial flight. The shield of the coat of arms of the United States signifies loyalty and devotion to duty.

III. **Award Eligibility: Army Aviator:** The individual must have satisfactorily completed the prescribed training and proficiency tests conducted by the U.S. Army Aviation Center and must have been designated as an Aviator in

V. **Subdued Badges:** Subdued badges are authorized in metal and cloth. The metal badge is black; the cloth badge is a base cloth with design elements embroidered in black.

VI. **Miniature Badges:** Dress miniature badges are authorized.

⭐ Flight Surgeon Badges, Group Three

Flight Surgeon

Senior Flight Surgeon

Master Flight Surgeon

I. **Description:** An oxidized silver badge 23/32 inch in height and 2 1/2 inches in width, consisting of a shield, its field scored with horizontal lines and bearing the Staff of Aesculapius on and over a pair of displayed wings. A star is added above the shield to indicate the degree of Senior Flight Surgeon and the star is surrounded with a laurel wreath to indicate the degree of Master Flight Surgeon.

II. **Symbolism:** The wings suggest flight and reflect the skills associated with aerial flight. The Staff of Aesculapius is traditionally and historically associated with healing and medical skills.

III. **Award Eligibility:** Awarded to any medically qualified Army Medical Corps Officer who satisfactorily completes training and other requirements prescribed in AR 600-105.

IV. **Date Approved:** The Flight Surgeon Badge *(originally approved as the Aviation Medical Officer Badge)* was approved on 28 December 1956. The Senior Flight Surgeon *(formerly the Flight Surgeon)* and Master Flight Surgeon *(formerly the Senior Flight Surgeon)* Badges were approved on 12 August 1963. The changes in designations were by message from the Commander, U.S. Army Military Personnel Center, 22 November 1973.

V. **Subdued Badges:** Subdued badges are authorized in metal and cloth. The metal badge is black. The cloth badge is a base cloth with design elements embroidered in black.

VI. **Miniature Badges:** Dress miniature badges are authorized in the following sizes: Flight Surgeon: 21/64 inch in height and 1 1/4 inches in width; Senior Flight Surgeon: 13/32 inch in height and 1 1/4 inches in width; Master Fight Surgeon: 15/32 inch in height and 1 1/4 inches in width.

⭐ Aircraft Crew Member Badges, Group Three

Aircraft Crew Member

Senior Aircraft Crew Member

Master Aircraft Crew Member

Subdued Badges

I. **Description:** An oxidized silver badge 3/4 inch in height and 2 1/2 inches in width, consisting of a shield with its field scored with horizontal lines and bearing the coat of arms of the United States on and over a pair of displayed wings. A star is added above the shield to indicate the degree of Senior Aircraft Crew Member and the star is surrounded with a laurel wreath to indicate the degree of Master Aircraft Crew Member.

II. **Symbolism:** The badge is the same design as that for Army Aviator with the coat of arms of the United States substituted for the shield of the coat of arms of the United States. The wings suggest flight and reflect the skills associated with aerial flight. The coat of arms of the United States on the shield signifies loyalty and devotion to duty.

III. **Award Eligibility:** The badges are awarded in degrees to personnel who have met the following requirements: Crew Member: Individual must be on flying status as a crew member in a specified position or non-crewmember in the case of observers, medical aidmen, gunners, aircraft maintenance supervisors or technical inspectors. Senior: Be recommended and on flying status as a crewmember or as a non-crewmember, performed 7 years in one of the principal duty assignments above, and attained grade E-4 or higher. Master: Be recommended and on flying status in a specified position or non-crewmember position, have performed 15 years in one or more of the principal duty assignments above and attained the grade of E-6 or higher. Personnel who have met the above requirements at any time since 1 January 1947 are eligible for these badges.

IV. **Date Approved:** Approved by the Deputy Chief of Staff for Military Operations on 16 May 1962.

V. **Subdued Badges:** Subdued badges are authorized in metal and cloth. The metal badge is black. The cloth badge is a base cloth with design elements embroidered in black.

VI. **Miniature Badges:** Dress miniature badges are authorized.

Explosive Ordnance Disposal Badge, Group Three

Basic EOD

Senior EOD

Master EOD

I. **Description:** A silver badge, 1 3/4 inches in height, consisting of shield charged with a conventional, drop bomb, point down, from which radiates four lightning flashes, all in front of and contained within a wreath of laurel leaves. The Senior Explosive Ordnance Disposal Badge is the same as the basic badge except the drop bomb bears a 7/32 inch silver star. The Master Explosive Ordnance Disposal Badge is the same as the Senior except a star, surrounded by a laurel wreath, is added above the shield.

II. **Symbolism:** The shield charged with a drop bomb is from the shoulder sleeve insignia approved for the Bomb Disposal School in 1942. The device was subsequently adopted for wear on a brassard to identify bomb disposal personnel. The bomb, with point down, indicates a live bomb and with the shield reflects the functions of ordnance personnel to safely dispose of live ordnance.

III. **Award Eligibility:** The specific criteria for award of the Explosive Ordnance Disposal Badges is included in AR 600-8-22, all badges require assignment to specific TOE/TDA EOD positions must be recommended by the commander.

   a. **Explosive Ordnance Disposal (EOD) Badge:** Must have MOS 55D (enlisted) or 91E (officer), complete prescribed instruction and perform satisfactorily for 18 months for the award to become permanent.

   b. **Senior Explosive Ordnance Disposal Badge:** Must have been awarded the basic EOD Badge and served 36 months in an EOD position following award of the basic badge.

   c. **Master Explosive Ordnance Disposal Badge:** Must have been awarded the Senior EOD Badge and served 60 months in a TOE/TDA officer of NCO EOD position, since award of the senior badge.

IV. **Date Approved:** The Chief of Staff, U.S. Army, approved the Explosive Ordnance Disposal Specialist and the Explosive Ordnance Disposal Supervisor Badges on 31 July 1957. In June 1969, the Master EOD Badge was authorized. At the same time, the designation of the supervisor's badge was changed to Senior EOD Badge and the EOD Specialist Badge was changed to EOD Badge.

Subdued Badge

V. **Subdued Badge:** The subdued badge is authorized in metal and cloth. The metal badges have a black finish

VI. **Miniature Badges:** A dress miniature badge, 7/8 inch wide, is authorized.

⭐ Parachutists Badge, Group Four

                Basic   Senior   Master

I. **Description:** An oxidized silver badge 1 13/64 inches in height and 1 1/2 inches in width, consisting of an open parachute on and over a pair of stylized wings displayed and curving inward. A star and wreath are added above the parachute canopy to indicate the degree of qualification. A star above the canopy indicates a Senior Parachutist; the star surrounded by a laurel wreath indicates a Master Parachutist. Small stars are superimposed on the appropriate badge to indicate combat jumps as shown below under combat Parachutist Badges:

II. **Symbolism:** The wings suggest flight and, together with the open parachute, symbolize individual proficiency and parachute qualifications.

III. **Award Eligibility:** Basic, Senior and Master Parachutist badges are awarded to individuals rated excellent in character and efficiency who have met the following requirements:

Basic Parachutist: Completed the proficiency test assigned to an airborne unit or the Airborne Department of the Infantry School or having one combat parachute jump.

Senior Parachutist: A minimum of 30 jumps to include 15 jumps with combat equipment; two night jumps, one as jumpmaster of a stick; two mass tactical jumps which culminate in an airborne assault problem; graduated from the Jumpmaster Course; and served on jump status with an airborne unit or other organization authorized parachutists for at least 24 months.

Master Parachutist: 65 jumps to include 25 jumps with combat equipment; four night jumps, one as a jumpmaster of a stick; five mass tactical jumps which culminate in an airborne assault problem with a battalion or larger; separate company/battery or organic staff of a regiment size or larger; graduated from the Jumpmaster Course; and served in jump status with an airborne unit or other organization authorized parachutists for a total of at least 36 months.

⭐ Combat Parachutist Badges, Group Four

  One Jump   Two Jumps   Three Jumps   Four Jumps   Five Jumps

A bronze service star is authorized to be worn on the parachute badge to denote a soldiers participation in a combat parachute jump. Orders are required to confirm award of the combat parachute badge. A soldier's combat parachute jump credit is tied directly to the combat assault credit decision for the unit to which the soldier is attached or assigned at the time of the assault. Each soldier must physically exit the aircraft to receive the combat parachute jump credit and the parachutist badge with bronze service star. *(Note: award of the combat parachutist badge qualifies the recipient to wear the bronze arrowhead for a combat assault on the campaign medal awarded for that service.)*

One jump: A bronze star centered on the shroud lines 3/16 inch below the canopy.

Two jumps: A bronze star on the base of each wing.

Three jumps: A bronze star on the base of each wing and one star centered on the shroud lines 3/16 inch below the canopy.

Four jumps: Two bronze stars on the base of each wing.

Five jumps: A gold star centered on the shroud lines 5/16 inch below the canopy.

Stars are shown on a master parachutist badge but would be placed on an individual's badge *(Basic, Senior or Master)*.

★ Pathfinder Badge, Group Four

I. **Description:** A gold color metal and enamel badge 1 3/16 inches in height and 1 1/2 inches in width, consisting of a gold sinister wing displayed on and over a gold torch with red and gray flames.

II. **Symbolism:** The wing suggests flight and airborne capabilities; the torch symbolizes leadership and guidance implying pathfinder combat skills.

III. **Award Eligibility:** The Commandant of the U.S. Army Infantry School may award the Pathfinder Badge for successfully completion of the Pathfinder Course.

IV. **Date Approved:** The badge was originally approved on 22 May 1964 in felt and replaced as a metal and enamel item on 11 October 1968.

V. **Subdued Badges:** A subdued badge in black metal finish of the same design is authorized.

VI. **Miniature Badges:** A dress miniature badge, 11/16 inch in height and 7/8 inch in width is authorized.

★ Ranger Qualification Tab

Ranger Qualification Patch

I. **Description:** The ranger qualification tab for the Army green uniform is 2 3/8 inches wide with a yellow embroidered border and letters over a black background. A subdued version with black letters and border on an olive drab background is authorized on battle dress uniforms.

II. **Symbolism:** The colors reflect the previously authorized ranger shoulder sleeve insignia which was diamond shaped with yellow border and letters and a deep blue background.

III. **Award Eligibility:**

a. The Commandant of the U.S. Army Infantry School awards the Ranger Tab to any person who successfully completed a Ranger Course conducted by that school.

IV. **Date Approved:** The cloth tab was approved by HQDA on 6 November 1950. Authorization to wear the tab was included in Change 2, AR 600-70, dated 23 January 1953. On 25 November 1984, the Army Chief of Staff approved a metal replica of the embroidered tab for wear on the dress mess uniforms.

V. **Subdued Tab:** The subdued tab is embroidered on a cloth background and bordered with black letters.

VI. **Miniature Badges:** The metal badge authorized for wear on the Army blue or white uniform and green shirt is 1 5/32 inches wide with a black enameled background and gold letters and border. The dress miniature for wear on the mess/dress uniforms is 13/16 inch wide.

★ The Jungle Expert Patch

The **Jungle Expert Patch** was often worn by graduates of the Jungle Operations Training Center (JOTC) until the school became inactive in 1999. The patch may have been authorized for wear by soldiers assigned to U.S. Army South who graduate from JOTC but the patch was never recognized Army-wide.

In 2014, the JOTC was reopened in Hawaii and the Jungle Expert Patch was revitalized as a tab authorized for soldiers who complete the course and are assigned to the U.S. Army Pacific. Other graduates receive the tab as a souvenir.

Current Jungle Expert Tab | Jungle Expert Patch

⭐ Driver and Mechanic Badges *(6 clasps)*

   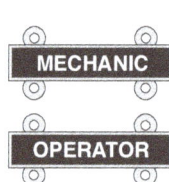 

I. **Description:** An oxidized silver cross pattee with a disk wheel and tire placed in the center. At the bottom of the cross are two rings for attaching qualification bars.

II. **Symbolism:** The cross stands for achievement in operations and the wheel symbolizes skill area.

III. **Award Eligibility:** The Driver and Mechanics Badge is awarded to soldiers who successfully complete the prescribed requirements:

Driver; have a U.S. Government motor operators card and 12 months or 8000 miles of accident free driving.

Mechanic; must pass standard mechanics course and demonstrated mechanical skills to justify such a rating.

Operator; a soldier whose primary duty is to operate Army material handling equipment or mechanical equipment for 12 months or 500 hours.

IV. **Date Approved:** This badge was authorized during World War II.

V. **Subdued Badge:** No subdued badge is authorized.

VI. **Miniature Badge:** No miniature badge is authorized.

⭐ Parachute Rigger Badge, Group Five

I. **Description:** A silver winged hemispherical canopy with conically arrayed cords, 1-3/4 inches wide, with a band centered on the badge inscribed "RIGGER".

II. **Symbolism:** The winged parachute represents the functions of rigging of supplies for air drop as well as packing and repair of parachutes used for personnel and cargo.

III. **Award Eligibility:** The Parachute Rigger Badge is awarded to soldiers who successfully complete the prescribed course of instruction conducted by the U.S. Army Quartermaster School and have been awarded MOS 43E *(enlisted)* or 401A *(warrant)*. Officers may be awarded the badge upon completion of a course of instruction.

IV. **Date Approved:** The Parachute Rigger Badge was approved by the Chief of Staff, U.S. Army, on 9 June 1968. This approval was retroactive to include personnel who completed the prescribed course of instruction subsequent to May 1951.

V. **Subdued Badge:** The subdued badge is authorized in metal and cloth. The metal badges have a black finish. The cloth badge is on a base cloth with the wings, canopy, ropes and letters embroidered in black. The designation band and background between the ropes are embroidered in olive drab.

VI. **Miniature Badge:** A dress miniature badge, 7/8 inch wide, is authorized.

⭐ Air Assault, Airmobile Badge, Obsolete

An earlier **Air Assault Badge**, was worn in the early 1960s by troops of 11th Airborne division who qualified for it by making three helicopter rappels from 60 feet and three from 120 feet. Soldiers were also required to be knowledgeable of aircraft safety procedures; familiar with aircraft orientation; proficient in hand and arm signals and combat assault operations;. The badge was first awarded in early 1964 and was only authorized for wear by soldiers within the 11th Airborne division, as it was a division award and not authorized for Army-wide wear by the Department of the Army.

⭐ Diver Badges, Group Five

  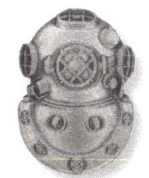  

Scuba **Salvage** **Second Class** **First Class** **Master**

The Army has two different types of diver badges, one for engineer divers and one for special operations divers. Army engineer diver badges are awarded in four degrees *(second-class diver, salvage diver, first-class diver, and master diver)* while Army special operations diver badges are awarded in two degrees *(diver and diving supervisor)*. The second-class and first-class diver badges are identical to those issued by U.S. Navy. Navy-awarded Diving Officer Insignia, Diving Medical Officer Insignia, and Diving Medical Technician Insignia are authorized for wear on Army uniforms with written approval from the United States Army Human Resources Command.

On 17 September 2004, the Scuba Diver Insignia/Badge was discontinued and replaced by the new Special Operations Diver Badge with an additional grade, the Special Operations Diving Supervisor Badge.

Scuba: A 1 inch high silver badge consisting of a scuba diver's hood with face mask, mouthpiece, and breathing tubes. The width is 31/32 inch. The distinctive equipment of the scuba diver represents the skills and abilities required to qualify for the basic diver rating.

Salvage: A silver diving helmet, 1 inch in height, with the letter "S" 3/8 inch in height, superimposed on the chest plate. The width is 23/32 inch. The diver's helmet is the basic equipment and the letter "S" is superimposed on the design to reflect salvage activities such as harbor clearance, rock and concrete blasting, steel and timber removal and the removal of propellers for replacement.

Second Class: A silver MK5 diving helmet 1 inch in height. The width is 23/32 inch. The diver's helmet is the basic equipment used in diving operations.

First Class: A silver MK5 diving helmet 15/16 inch in height, between two dolphins, 1 inch high. The width is 1 3/32 inches. The badge includes the design of the diver's helmet to reflect diving operations and includes the dolphins to suggest the function of diving, without the helmet required of a deep sea diver.

Master: A silver MK5 diving helmet 7/8 inch in height in front of a trident 1 1/4 inches in height between two dolphins. The width is 1 3/32 inches. The trident is added to the design of the First Class badge which is symbolic of a marine spearhead and stands for valor and strength.

The Second Class, Salvage, First Class and Master Diver Badges were approved on 15 February 1944.

Subdued Badges: Subdued badges are authorized in metal and cloth. The metal badge for all designs is black.

⭐ Marksmanship Badges

U.S. Army Distinguished Rifleman Badge

Awarded to Army personnel in recognition for outstanding achievement in competitive target practice firing with the military service rifle; the award requires a specified number of points (30) attained from competition matches, basically this meant winning three team badges. The Badge is gold, shield-shaped with a black and white target in the center; the shield is attached to a suspension bar that contains the words "U.S. Army." The reverse is blank for engraving of the recipient's name and date of award.

U.S. Army Distinguished Pistol Shot Badge

Army personnel are recognized for outstanding achievement in competitive target practice firing with the military service pistol with the Distinguished Pistol Shot Badge; the award requires a specified number of points *(30)* attained from competition matches. Usually awarded to a winner of three team badges. It is a gold, shield-shaped badge with a black and white target in the center and the words "U.S. Army" on the suspension bar.

Badges for Marksmanship

The current **Expert** qualification badges are authorized for qualified personnel of the Army, Army Reserve, and National Guard is made of oxidize silver. World War II versions were made of sterling silver but today it is a white metal *(silver, nickel and rhodium)*, 1.17 inches in height, a cross patee with the representation of a target placed on the center and enclosed by a wreath of laurel leaves tied at the bottom with a knot. It has two rings at the bottom for attaching a bar naming the weapon with which the recipient qualified.

Sharpshooter qualification badge are authorized for qualified personnel of the Army, Army Reserve, and National Guard. World War II versions are made of sterling silver but today it is a white metal *(silver, nickel, and rhodium)*, 1 inch in height, a cross patee with the representation of a target placed on the center. It has two rings at the bottom for attaching a bar naming the weapon with which the recipient qualified.

Marksman qualification badge are authorized for qualified personnel of the Army, Army Reserve, and National Guard. World War II versions were made of sterling silver but today it is a white metal *(silver, nickel, and rhodium)*, 1 inch in height, a cross patee. It has two rings at the bottom for attaching a bar naming the weapon with which the recipient qualified.

Before WW II, qualification dates were often engraved on the back of bars.

Weapons qualification bars: Originally of sterling silver these bars of white metal have rings at the top for attaching to the Expert, Sharpshooter and Marksmanship qualification badge or to the last previously earned bar. Qualification Bars: Bars with the following inscriptions are currently authorized for display on the badges:

- Rifle, Machine Gun, Submachine Gun, Rocket Launcher, Small Bore Pistol, Pistol, Field Artillery, Grenade, Mortar, Missile, AA Artillery, Tank Weapons, Carbine, Bayonet, Aeroweapons, Auto Rifle, Flamethrower, Recoilless Rifle and Small Bore Rifle.

Prior to 1951 regulation, the titles of the badges were Marksman and 2d Class Gunner; Sharpshooter and First Class Gunner and Expert.

IDENTIFICATION BADGES

⭐ Presidential Service Identification Badge

The **Presidential Service Badge** was established on September 1, 1964. It replaced the White House Service Badge which had been established on June 1, 1960. A replica of the Presidential Coat of Arms is superimposed on a dark blue enameled disk surrounded by 27 gold rays radiating from the center. It is given by the President to Armed Forces personnel assigned to duty in the White House office or to military units and support facilities under the administration of the Military Assistant to the President for a period of at least one year, after January 20, 1961, as recognition, in a permanent way, of their contribution in the service of the President. Once earned, the badge becomes a permanent part of the recipient's uniform, and may be worn after the recipient leaves Presidential service.

Presidential Service Badge

⭐ Vice-Presidential Service Identification Badge

Old Vice Presidential Service Badge

Current Vice Presidential Service Badge

The **Vice-Presidential Service Badge** was established on July 8, 1970. The seal of the Vice-President of the United States is superimposed on a white enameled disc surrounded by 27 gold rays radiating from the center. The badge is awarded in the name of the Vice-President to members of the armed forces who have been assigned to duty in the Office of the Vice-President for a period of at least one year after January 20, 1969. Once earned, the badge becomes a permanent part of the uniform.

⭐ Office of the Secretary of Defense Identification Badge

The **Office of the Secretary of Defense Identification Badge** is a military badge issued to members of the United States armed forces who are permanently assigned to the Office of the Secretary of Defense (OSD) and its subordinate offices, and in addition, to some of the Defense Agencies and Department of Defense Field Activities.

The badge was first created in 1949 and was referred to as the *"National Military Establishment Identification Badge."* In 1950, the badge was renamed as *"Department of Defense Identification Badge."* On December 20, 1962 the badge was given its current name. It is issued as a permanent decoration and is to be worn for the remainder of an individual's military career, provided that a service member served at least one year *(two years for Reserve personnel not on active duty)* in or in support of OSD. Army personnel are awarded the badge when they are assigned on a permanent basis to any of the The Offices of the Secretary of Defense The badge, 2 inches in diameter, consists of an eagle with wings spread grasping three crossed arrows on its breast a shield paleways of thirteen pieces argent and gules a chief azure, a gold annulet passing behind the wing tips bearing thirteen gold stars above the eagle and a wreath of laurel and olive in green enamel below the eagle, the whole superimposed on a silver sunburst of 33 rays.

★ Joint Chiefs of Staff Identification Badge

The **Office of the Joint Chiefs of Staff Identification Badge** is a United States military badge authorized members of the Joint Chiefs of Staff upon appointment to position as either a Service Head, Vice Chairman, or Chairman of the Joint Chiefs of Staff. The badge is also authorized staff and support personnel assigned to the Office of the Chairman and the Joint Staff. Individuals may qualify for permanent wear of this badge after being assigned for one year on active duty or two years as a reservist. The badge is an oval silver metal wreath of laurel, 2 1/4 inches in height and 2 inches in width overall, the shield of the United States *(the chief in blue enamel and the 13 stripes alternating white and red enamel)* superimposed on four gold metal unsheathed swords, two in pale and two in saltire with points to chief, the points and pommels resting on the wreath, the blades and grips entwined with a gold metal continuous scroll surrounding the shield with the word JOINT at the top and the words CHIEFS OF STAFF at the bottom, all in blue enamel letters. Laurel is symbolic of achievement, courage, and victory. The four unsheathed swords refer to the armed might of the Army, Navy, Air Force, and Marine Corps and their combined constant vigilance and readiness in the defense of the United States.

The Office of the Joint Chiefs of Staff Identification Badge was first approved in February 1963 and has remained unchanged in appearance since then.

★ Army Staff Identification Badge

The **Army Staff Identification Badge** is a badge worn by personnel who serve at the Office of the Secretary of the Army and the Army Staff at Headquarters, Department of the Army *(HQDA)* and its agencies. The badge is a distinguishing emblem of service. Initially issued as a temporary badge, officers and enlisted personnel demonstrating outstanding performance of duty and meeting all eligibility requirements can be processed after one complete year *(365 days cumulative)* of assignment and receive a certificate authorizing permanent wear of the badge.

General Douglas MacArthur first proposed an Army General Staff Badge in 1931, but it was not until 1933 that the United States War Department authorized it. The name was changed in 1982 from the Army General Staff Identification Badge to the Army Staff Identification Badge. On the Army uniform, the Badge is worn centered on the right breast pocket; however, wear of the Badge is authorized on the left breast pocket when worn in conjunction with a deployment CSIB *(Combat Service Identification Badge)*.

★ Guard of the Unknown Soldier Identification Badge

The **Guard of the Unknown Soldier identification badge** is authorized by the Commanding Officer, First Battalion, Third Infantry, for wear by each member of the Guard, Tomb of the Unknown Soldier, during their assignment of duty. Effective 17 December, 1963, the Commanding Officer, First Battalion, Third Infantry, may authorize the wearing of the badge as a permanent badge for soldiers who have served honorably a minimum of nine months and who are recommended by the Commander of the Honor Guard company, First Battalion *(Reinforced)*, Third Infantry *(the Old Guard)*. The Identification Badge, Guard of the Tomb of the Unknown Soldier is a beautifully designed silver metal badge for wear on the right breast pocket of the uniform. It is made of frosted and cut silver with the highlights polished. The design is an inverted wreath of laurel and olive leaves intertwined at the top of the badge. In the center of the wreath is a replica of the of the tomb of the Unknown Soldier resting on a platform with the words Honor Guard. This award is retroactive to 1 February 1958 for personnel on active duty.

⭐ Drill Sergeant Identification Badge

The **Drill Sergeant identification badge** is awarded for successful completion of the Drill Sergeant course and assignment as a drill sergeant to a training command.

The Commandant of the Drill Sergeant school can authorize the permanent wear of the badge to eligible personnel by letter. Officers are authorized to wear this badge if it was permanently awarded to them while in an enlisted status. It is worn on the lower part of the right side breast pocket of the Class A uniform.

The badge may be revoked if the recipient is removed from the position of a Drill Sergeant for cause, regardless of the amount of time the individual has served in the position in a satisfactory manner. Authority to revoked the badge is delegated to Commanders of U.S. Army Training Centers and Commandant of the drill sergeant schools. Commanders of U.S. Army Training Centers may further delegate the revocation authority to commanders in the grade of Colonel or higher who have the authority to remove soldiers from Drill Sergeant duties and withdraw the skill qualification identifier.

⭐ U.S. Army Recruiter Identification Badge

The **U.S. Army Basic Recruiter Badge** is authorized for wear by military personnel assigned to Recruiting Commands designated by the Commanding General, U. S. Army Recruiting Command. Officers are authorized to wear this badge if it was permanently awarded to them while in an enlisted status.

Gold Achievement Stars: 1, 2 or 3 gold achievement stars may be awarded for meeting the criteria set by Recruiting Command. The stars will be affixed to the basic badge.

The **Commanding General, Recruiting Command** may authorize the wear of the basic recruiter's badge as a permanent part of the uniform for qualified enlisted personnel and commanders who honorably completed their tour of duty in recruiting on or after 1 July 1980.

U. S. Army Gold Recruiter Badge and sapphire achievement stars are authorized by Recruiting Command for wear by eligible members who meet established criteria. This award is retroactive to January 1975 for personnel on active duty. The Gold Recruiter's Badge can be authorized as a permanent part of the uniform for eligible personnel by the Commanding General, U.S. Army Recruiting Command.

The **Career Counselors Badge** may be authorized for wear by enlisted personnel assigned to authorized duty positions which require the military occupational specialty 00E or 79 delta, including personnel assigned to U.S. Army Recruiting Command. The award is retroactive to 1 January 1972. The badge is authorized for temporary wear only and will be withdrawn when the awardee is reassigned or ceases to perform the require duties of MOS 00E or 79 delta satisfactorily.

The Career Counselors Badge may be authorized for wear by enlisted members of the Army Reserve who have successfully completed the Resident or Nonresident Reserve Component Recruiting Course and had been designated as U. S. Army Reserve Reenlistment Noncommissioned Officers. The badge is authorized for temporary wear only and will be withdrawn when the awardee ceases to be a designated U.S. Army Reserve Reenlistment Noncommissioned Officer.

⭐ U.S. Army Reserve Recruiter Badge

The U.S. Army Reserve Recruiter Badge is authorized for wear by qualified members of the U.S. Army Reserve who had been designated by letter as an Army Reserve Recruiter. Wear of the badge as a uniform item is announced by the Commanders of Army Reserve General Officer Commands. Authority to wear this badge is withdrawn when the awardee is released from recruiting duty, although it may be retained as a memento of successful completion of assigned recruiting duties.

⭐ National Guard Recruiter Badge

The Army National Guard Recruiter's Badge may be authorized for wear by enlisted personnel assigned to authorized National Guard duty positions which require military occupational specialty 00E or 79 delta, including personnel assigned to the United States Army Recruiting Command. Authority to wear this badge is withdrawn when the awardee is released from recruiting duty, although it may be retained as a memento of successful completion of assigned recruiting duties.

Master gold with wreath

⭐ U.S. Army Military Police Badge

The U.S. Army Military Police Badge is authorized for wear by qualified members of the U.S. Army Military Police who had been designated as Military Police and completed the prescribed course of training. Wear of the badge as a uniform item is announced by the Military Police Commanders. Authority to wear this badge is withdrawn when the awardee is released from Military Police duty. The badge is an official symbol of their office.

Military Police Badge

Examples of Foreign Badges Authorized for Wear on the Right Breast

South Vietnamese Army Parachute Badge

South Vietnamese Ranger Badge

South Vietnamese Special Forces Parachute Badge

French Army Parachute Badge

⭐ Overseas Service Bars

The Overseas Service Bar is an Army decoration displayed as an embroidered gold bar worn horizontally on the right sleeve of the U.S. Army Class A uniform. Called an Overseas Chevron in the First World War, it was an inverted chevron sewed on the lower left uniform sleeve. In 1918, the Overseas Chevron design was identical to the Wound Chevron worn on the right sleeve. In World War II, the Overseas Chevron was redesignated as the Overseas Bar and designed as a horizontal bar. Veterans of both the First and Second World Wars wore both the Overseas Bar and Chevron together.

During the Vietnam War, the Overseas Service Bar was worn on the lower right sleeve, instead of the left. Today an Overseas Service Bar is awarded for each 6 months overseas in a combat zone. Overseas time is cumulative, therefore one bar can be awarded for two 3 month deployments. Soldiers can be awarded multiple Overseas Service Bars for several years spent in an overseas combat zone. Multiple Overseas Service Bars are worn vertically on the right sleeve of the uniform. The Overseas Service Bar is a separate decoration from the Overseas Service Ribbon however soldiers can receive both awards for the same period of service.

Overseas Service Bars

⭐ Service Stripes

A service stripe, traditionally called a hash mark by soldiers, is worn by enlisted soldiers to denote length of service. The Army awards each stripe for three years service. The concept of a service stripe goes back to the Civil War where sleeve stripes marked completion of a standard enlistment. Soldiers wear them on the left sleeve and Overseas Service Bars on the right one. Service stripes are only worn on class A uniforms.

A service stripe is presented to an enlisted soldier upon completion of the specified term of service, regardless of the soldier's disciplinary history. A soldier with non-judicial punishments or court-martials will still receive a service stripe for three years service but the Good Conduct Medal would be denied.

⭐ Infantry Blue Shoulder Cord

Officers and enlisted men of the Infantry who have been awarded the Combat Infantryman Badge or Expert Infantryman Badge or have completed the basic infantry training courses wear the infantry blue shoulder cord on the right shoulder of the Army dress and full dress uniform. The cord goes under the arm and attaches to a regulation small U.S. Army button attached to the shoulder seam 1/2 inch outside the right collar edge.

Other Great Medals and Insignia Books All Available at WWW.MOAPress.com or on Amazon

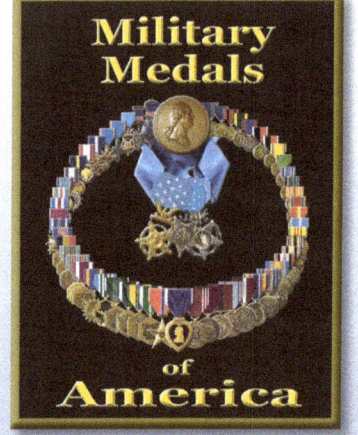
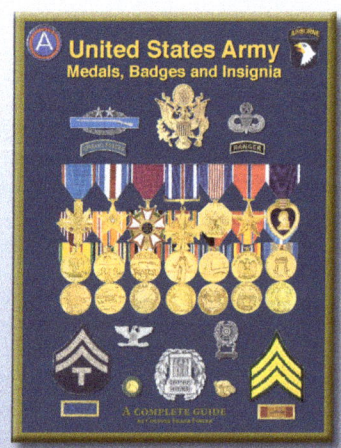

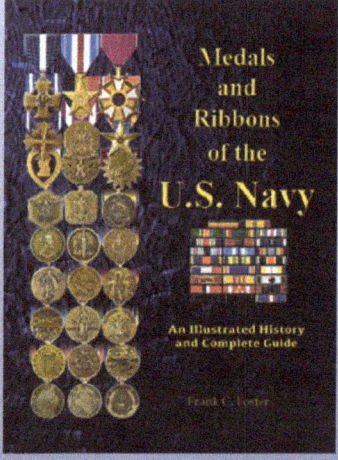
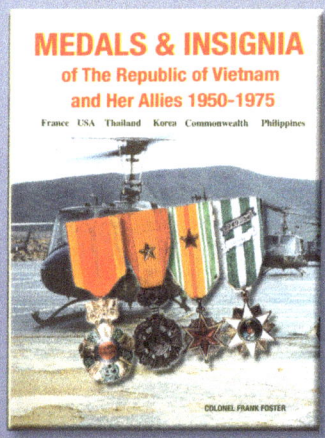
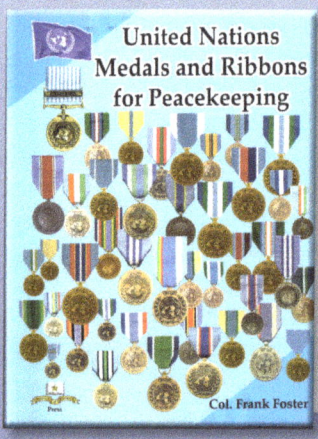
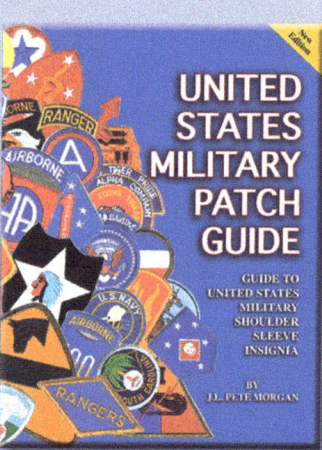

America's Best Medal and Ribbon Wear Guides All Available at WWW.MOAPress.com or on Amazon

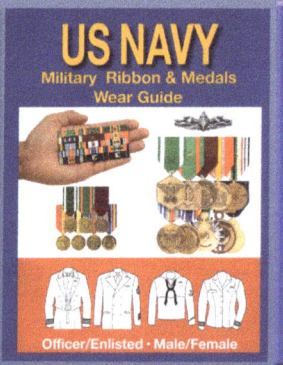

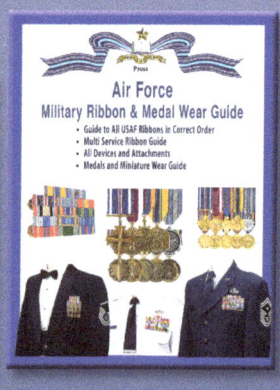

48 Insignia, Rank and Badges, U.S. Army Vietnam

www.ingramcontent.com/pod-product-compliance
Lightning Source LLC
Chambersburg PA
CBHW051320110526
44590CB00031B/4422